Bible Gems

Bible Gems

by

Ivor Powell

KREGEL PUBLICATIONS
Grand Rapids, Michigan 49501

Bible Gems, by Ivor Powell. © 1987 by Kregel Publications, a division of Kregel, Inc., P. O. Box 2607, Grand Rapids, Michigan 49501. First Kregel Publications edition: 1987.

Library of Congress Cataloging-in-Publication Data

Powell, Ivor, 1910-
Bible Gems.

Includes index
1. Bible–Meditations. I. Title.
BX491.5.P67 1987 220.6 86-27525

ISBN 0-8254-3527-7

2 3 4 5 6 Printing/Year 94 93 92 91 90

Printed in the United States of America

CONTENTS

PREFACE

My first Bible book, *Bible Cameos*, was published in 1951 and was followed by four others of its type. They were written to help ministers. It is with gratitude to God that I now remember how He graciously blessed those volumes. They went around the world bringing inspiration to many people, and some of the books were translated into Japanese, Telagu, German, and French. I shall always treasure a letter which came from a leprosarium in India. One of the doctors had read *Bible Pinnacles* and wished to thank me for the inspiration received.

The publication of a book resembles the launching of a ship or a balloon; it is impossible to know where it may travel before its ministry is completed. Let me confess that the reason for the writing of *Bible Gems* is the same as that which motivated the writing of its predecessors. When I was a pastor of a church in Wales, my Saturday nights were often distressing. Many activities during the week stole my time, and I became anxious when the sermons for Sunday were elusive. All ministers know the experience. It is my sincere prayer that this volume will join the earlier books in assisting pastors worldwide.

Readers of the earlier volumes will discover an additional feature in this book. I have included what may be termed four *miniseries* of Bible studies. This has been done to offer increased assistance to pastors as they expound the Word of God in their Sunday and midweek services. For example, there is a collection of studies which deals with the Minor Prophets, and within that series is a shorter one expounding the experiences of Jonah. Special attention has been given to the Epistle to the Hebrews, where important themes have been likened to freeways running through a country. Finally, a progression of studies relates to the seven churches of Asia. It is hoped these messages will be of surpassing interest to ministers as they prepare their preaching programs.

I am indebted to my publisher's talented staff who are responsible for the production of my books. They make each publication an object of beauty. I am grateful to my wife, Betty, for her patience and skill in editing my work. However careful I am in the perusal of the material, her keen eyes always find errors which I did not see. I thank Mrs. Eleanor Dzuro, who typed the manuscript as a service for her Lord. It took a whole year to write this book, but if pastors become more efficient in their work for the Savior, my efforts will have been wonderfully rewarded.

IVOR POWELL

Santa Barbara, California

GOD . . . who restored a lost planet

(GENESIS 1:1-3)

"In the beginning GOD." That simple statement represents the greatest utterance ever made by man. No one knows when God created the universe. Many and varied have been the opinions expressed; innumerable discussions have been held, but whenever that beginning took place, God was there! He was the source of everything good. The Lord was the Supreme Architect, for He designed the heavens and earth. God was the creator of matching colors, for He made the flowers to blend with green grass. He matched green trees with blue skies and, when autumn arrived, contrived to make bare branches harmonize with darkening clouds. God created variety, for He made innumerable animals and insects, and they were all different. He implanted within human beings the capacity to love, even as He loved.

Yet, God was confronted by a problem. Something had gone wrong with His beautiful creation; the original earth had become a waste and void, and the conclusion had to be "an enemy hath done this." Isaiah the prophet said, "For thus saith the LORD that created the heavens: God himself that formed the earth and made it; he hath established it, he created it *not in vain* — [*a void*] — he formed it to be inhabited: I am the LORD; and there is none else" (Isa. 45:18). Many teachers believe the cataclysmic disaster that befell the earth was the result of judgment upon Lucifer who rebelled against God. (See Isa. 14:12-15.) When God restored the earth, His method became the prototype of all evangelism.

"And the Spirit of God moved upon the face of the waters."

The Holy Spirit has always been the agency through whom God brought order out of chaos, beauty out of ugliness, sanity out of madness. Little is known about the original earth, and we are unable to comprehend the repulsiveness of anything destroyed by evil. It remains inconceivable that God could have created something ugly or imperfect. To behold the ruin of the planet earth filled God's heart with sadness, and yet at the same time it presented a challenge of great magnitude. Should He abandon it eternally, or should He begin the task of restoring its earlier beauty? That immense problem was second in importance to a greater task soon to confront the Almighty. His beloved people would also be marred by evil; sin would dominate the human heart where peace and happiness were meant to be predominant. Yet God never abandoned anyone who could be reclaimed. The work of the Holy Spirit was always evidence that God had commenced a salvage operation.

"And God said...."

"The entrance of thy words giveth light" (Ps. 119:130). Isaiah recognized the power of the Word of God when he wrote: "So shall my word be that goeth forth out of my mouth: it shall not return unto me void, but it shall accomplish that which I please, and it shall prosper in the thing whereto I sent it" (Isa. 55:11). The Holy Spirit's application of the Word of God to a ruined earth initiated transformations beyond imagination. Identical words applied by the *same* Spirit to the barren souls of men and women achieve similar results. "Old things are passed away; behold, all things are become new" (2 Cor. 5:17). No man should underestimate the effectiveness of the Word of God; it can accomplish the impossible. That is the reason why every prophet prefaced his remarks with the statement: "Thus saith the LORD." Paul often claimed that the gospel was the power of God unto salvation. Throughout the ages, darkened souls were illuminated because God's Word performed miracles of re-creation. The picture supplied in the restoration of the ruined earth only reflected the greater glory of redemption within the hearts of sinful men and women.

"And God said, let there be light: and there was light."

Probably the greatest event that can take place within humans is the illumination of the darkened chambers of the mind. Paul wrote "The god of this world hath blinded the minds of them which believe not, lest the light of the glorious gospel of Christ, who is the image of God, should shine unto them" (2 Cor. 4:4). When Adam and Eve were placed upon the restored earth, everything they needed awaited them. God knew then, and He knows now, how to care for His children. Unfortunately, our first parents failed to appreciate this fact, and alas, we have emulated their example. It is thrilling to know that, although we may displease God, we cannot destroy His love. "In the beginning God"; in the end, CHRIST. (See Rev. 22:21.) Within the Bible all roads lead to the Savior.

THE LAMB . . . whose story is everlasting

Many magnificent themes are to be found within the Scriptures, but the greatest of them concerns the Lamb of God who came to redeem sinful people. That message never grows old!

The Lamb in God's planning (Rev. 13:8)

"The Lamb slain from the foundation of the world." As we contemplate this immense subject, we resemble small children trying to understand the complexities of a computer. It is beyond comprehension that before time began the members of the Trinity foresaw the need of sinful people and planned how that need should be met. He who placed the worlds in space would eventually come to earth to die for sinners.

The Lamb in God's provision (Gen. 3:21)

There was neither joy nor noise in the Garden of Eden; even the birds were silent! Adam and Eve had sinned. A temporary eclipse of their sun had plunged joyous spirits into gloom. The voice of God had struck terror to their souls, and the burden of guilt had become too heavy to carry. Bewildered, they fled from the presence of the Lord, only to discover they were unable to silence the murmurings of their conscience. Their garments had become transparent; they were naked! They became aware of an outstretched hand; God was offering a gift; it was a coat made from the skin of a sacrificed animal. It was almost too good to be true!

The Lamb with God's patriarch (Gen. 22:13)

Isaac was relieved and astonished. He could hardly believe his eyes! A few moments earlier Abraham had stretched forth his hand to slay his son, but then came the ominous command, "STOP!" "And Abraham lifted up his eyes, and looked, and behold behind him a ram caught in a thicket by his horns; and Abraham went and took the ram, and offered him up for a burnt offering in the stead of his son." It was unbelievable. Possibly, as he returned to his home, Isaac continued to say, "That ram died in my place."

The Lamb with God's people (Exod. 12:13)

It was a night to be remembered. Pharaoh, the ruler of Egypt, was furious; his subjects were apprehensive; his slaves were jubilant. Moses had confidently predicted their prison doors were about to open; their chains would soon belong to their past. They were to slay a lamb and if necessary share it with neighbors. The blood had to be placed on the doorposts and lintels of their houses, for that night the angel of God would be passing through the land. He would be looking for the scarlet symbol that reflected the faith of the people.

The Lamb with God's preacher (John 1:29)

The eyes of John the Baptist were glowing. He was looking at the Lamb of God. He had preached to large audiences and had known the compelling power of the Holy Spirit, but this sight superseded all else. His heart seemed to be bursting when he cried, "Behold the Lamb of God, which taketh away the sin of the world." John saw beyond the narrow limitations of Israel's faith. This Lamb would be sufficient for every person on earth.

The Lamb in God's presentation (John 19:5-14)

Pilate was at a loss for words. What more could he say? He had said, "Behold the man" and "Behold your king," but the listeners had angrily rejected his presentations. Poor man! Had his soul been filled with faith, he could have emulated John's example and said, "Behold your Lamb." Alas, he had neither faith nor hope. He could hardly present that of which he knew nothing. Yet in some mysterious way, God was doing what Pilate could not. He was presenting the Lamb of God who was about to die for undeserving people.

The Lamb in God's presence (Heb. 2:9)

Many of the early church members were dismayed; things were not proceeding according to their plans. Saints were becoming martyrs, and the future was ominous. What could they believe in those distressing times? One of their number decided to tell them. " . . . but we see Jesus." In so many words, he went on to say that many things may be beyond our comprehension, but we can still see our Savior interceding for us at the right hand of the Majesty on high. "Let us therefore come boldly unto the throne of grace, that we may obtain mercy, and find grace to help in time of need" (Heb. 4:16).

The Lamb in God's palaces (Rev. 5:6)

John was very sad; a problem had arisen in heaven, and apparently no person could solve it. Describing the scene, he said, "One of the elders saith unto me, Weep not. . . . And I beheld, and, lo, in the midst of the throne . . . stood a Lamb as it had been slain. . . . And I beheld, and I heard . . . ten thousand times ten thousand, and thousands of thousands, Saying with a loud voice, Worthy is the Lamb that was slain" (Rev. 5:5-12). From everlasting to everlasting, God's delight was in the Lamb. Happy shall we be if we follow the divine example.

ABRAHAM . . . whose life was studied by Paul

(ROMANS 5:1; 5:9)

The message preached by Paul was so revolutionary that his listeners believed him to be a heretic. The entire theology of Israel was based on the fact that God had spoken through Moses, and what had been said was irrefutable and unchangeable. Paul disagreed and challenged his critics with statements which he claimed to be more important than any law spoken by Moses. They were almost speechless when he asked, "Why call ye Abraham your father?" They quoted Moses, but revered Abraham. Paul insisted that Abraham was justified by faith and not by works. Righteousness had been imputed to Abraham long before circumcision and the law were mentioned. Paul asked, "If salvation and righteousness depend on circumcision, how then could Abraham or anyone else be righteous without circumcision?" His arguments were very irritating.

The promise of a Son (Gen. 15:1-6)

Abraham had no child; furthermore, it appeared it would remain so. Then God gave to him a great promise. "And [God] brought him forth abroad, and said, Look now toward heaven, and tell the stars, if thou be able to number them: and he said unto him, *So shall thy seed be.* And [Abram] believed in the LORD; and *he counted it to him for righteousness.*" Long before Moses was born, the patriarch heard the promise of God, and it was faith that won God's commendation. Abraham was considered to be righteous. He was a sinner, but faith overshadowed his guilt, and he became the friend of God. (See 2 Chron. 20:7 and Jas. 2:23.) Paul insisted: "And therefore it was imputed to him for righteousness. Now it was not written for his sake alone, that it was imputed to him, *but for us also,* to whom it shall be imputed, if we believe on him that raised up Jesus our Lord from the dead; Who was delivered for our offences, and was raised again for our justification" (Rom. 4:22-25).

The pleasure of a saint (Gen. 18:1-15)

God always honors His promises; answers to prayer may be delayed, but the end result is never in doubt. Paul said, "[Abraham] against hope believed in hope, that he might become the father of many nations, according to that which was spoken, So shall thy seed be. And being not weak in faith, he considered not his own body now dead, when he was about an hundred years old, neither yet the deadness of Sarah's womb: He staggered not at the promise of God through unbelief; but was strong in faith, giving glory to God; And being fully persuaded that, what he had promised, he was able also to perform. And therefore it was imputed to him for righteousness"

(Rom. 4:18-22). The story of how God sent angels to Abraham's tent to repeat the promise, and of the laughter of Sarah, makes enjoyable reading. "And the LORD said unto Abraham, Wherefore did Sarah laugh? . . . Is any thing too hard for the LORD?" (Gen. 18:14). Obviously any person who is an intimate friend of God enjoys excellent company. Even a home can become filled with ecstasy when God sends His special servants to enlighten, encourage, and instruct His chosen servant.

The perception in a sacrifice (Gen. 22:5)

Seen from any viewpoint, the slaying of a son would have been a difficult task for any father. To plunge a dagger into the chest of Isaac would be a terrible experience. Yet, it appears from the Scripture that this was not the case with Abraham. Apparently, he had no fears; he looked not at the proposed sacrifice but at the unfailing promises of God. If Isaac remained dead, then God could never fulfill what had been promised. A corpse could not beget children. Perhaps some details mystified the patriarch, but of one thing he remained confident. If Isaac should die on Mount Moriah, God would raise him from the dead. Therefore he said to the servants, "Abide ye here with the ass; and I and the lad will go yonder and worship, *and come again to you.*" Amplifying this ancient truth, the writer to the Hebrews said: "By faith Abraham, when he was tried, offered up Isaac. . . . Accounting that God was able to raise him up, even from the dead" (Heb. 11:17-19). Abraham enjoyed peace when he walked with his God; God experienced pleasure when He walked with His friend. Obviously they enjoyed each other's company.

These were the vital details used by Paul when he preached about the value of faith in God. Faith had preceded the law and circumcision. A man was justified by what *he believed* and not by *what he did.* The law exposed sin; faith removed it. It has been claimed that JUSTIFIED means *Just-if-I'd* never sinned! Paul's theology was condensed into a few sentences. He wrote: "What shall we say then that Abraham our father . . . if Abraham were justified by works, he hath whereof to glory; *but not before God* . . . Abraham *believed* God, and it was counted unto him for righteousness" (Rom. 4:1-3). So will it also be with those whose confidence is in Christ.

MELCHIZEDEK . . . who never had any parents

(GENESIS 14:18-20)

The ancient priest Melchizedek was the most mysterious man mentioned in the Bible. As quickly as he came, he disappeared and was never seen again. His story is astonishing, but all who carefully study the details are thrilled by its content.

The strange priest from nowhere (Gen. 14:18-20)

After the liberation of Lot, Abram "brought back all the goods, and also brought again his brother Lot, and his goods, and the women also, and the people. . . . And Melchizedek king of Salem brought forth bread and wine: and he was the priest of the most high God." Hebrews 7:3 says he was "without father, without mother, without descent, having neither beginning of days, nor end of life; but made like unto the Son of God; abideth a priest continually." This statement is amazing. Abram was returning triumphantly from his battle with five kings, when suddenly he saw this strange person coming toward him. Melchizedek must have been dignified, serene, pleasant to behold, and commanding attention. When Abram took the spoils of war to give tithes to the stranger, he did something new. Tithes were only given to God. If Melchizedek had neither beginning nor ending, he could not have been human! If he never had a father nor mother, how did his life on earth begin? These questions have been asked throughout history. The Bible teaches there were occasions when God was manifested in the flesh, when God appeared in human form. These manifestations were known as *theophanies;* the Scriptures mention several of them. For example, read Judges 13 and compare verse 18 with Isaiah 9:6. "And the angel of the LORD said unto him, Why askest thou thus after my name, seeing it is secret?" The word translated *secret* means "wonderful." There is every reason to believe that the Lord came down to meet Abram as he returned from the battlefield.

The serene potentate from somewhere (Heb. 7:9)

"To whom also Abram gave a tenth part of all; first being by interpretation King of righteousness, and after that also King of Salem, which is King of peace." These statements are shrouded in mystery. There are people who believe that colonies of heavenly beings were upon the earth in the early days of human history and that the Son of God actually ruled over some, or all of them. However there is no conclusive evidence to support the assertion. Yet the writer to the Hebrews seemed to be well informed when he wrote his book. Were the names merely indicative of the realm to which Melchizedek belonged? Were they given that men would know the eternal kingdom of God was based on righteousness? We may never know the answer to these questions, but one thing becomes obvious. Melchizedek was unique — He was one of a kind. He was the only royal priest ever to walk the earth and therefore, if for no other reason, was a type of Christ, the King of glory. Yet it must never be forgotten that he might have been the Son of the living God; otherwise, who authorized him to receive tithes?

The simple message for everywhere (Heb. 7:21-25)

"(Thou art a priest for ever after the order of Melchizedek:) By so much was Jesus made a surety of a better testament. . . . But this man, because he continueth ever, hath an unchangeable priesthood. Wherefore he is able also to save them to the uttermost that come unto God by him, seeing he ever liveth to make intercession for them." Some people have difficulties understanding and explaining the mysteries surrounding the appearance and departure of the ancient priest, but no one should ever encounter problems appreciating the message expressed in the letter to the Hebrews. Men may not understand where Melchizedek came from, but all should know the origin of the Savior. "In the beginning was the Word, and the Word was with God, and the Word was God. . . . And the Word was made flesh and dwelt among us" (John 1:1,14). Readers may not know where Melchizedek ultimately went, but all should be aware of what Jesus said prior to His departure from this planet. He said, "I go to prepare a place for you. And if I go and prepare a place for you, I will come again, and receive you unto myself; that where I am, there ye may be also" (John 14:2-3). Christians cannot bow at the feet of Abram's priest — or can they? We may not be able to offer to him a tenth of our possessions — or can we? If the ancient figure was only a type of Christ, then we can rejoice because we have the Lord Himself. If he were indeed the Christ, then, as Abram of old, we can enjoy excellent company! This is a message of superlative worth, it should be proclaimed worldwide.

GOD . . . who sometimes moved very slowly

Impatience has been one of my greatest weaknesses. In my impetuosity, I have often thought I could drive my car a hundred miles before God could start His engine! Then, ten miles down the road when He found and lifted me from a ditch, I asked "What took you so long?" It always seemed strange that although God took only six days to create the world, He sometimes took six years to answer my prayers. Many of the delays of God are described in the Bible, but for the purpose of this study, only four incidents will be considered. Each one has a distinctive charm.

Methuselah . . . the delay to proclaim His mercy (Gen. 5:27)

Long ago when the world was young, when foreign countries were unknown and the inhabitants of the earth lived in a very small area, there lived a man called Enoch. He was not a recluse, but he loved to walk in the country with God; he appreciated excellent company! When he was sixty-five years of age, his wife gave birth to their first child, and the gift changed the father's life. Prior to the arrival of the baby, Enoch *lived;* after he "*walked with God*." (See Gen. 5:21-22.) Possibly the mother was surprised when the father called his son Methuselah. The name had never previously been given, and probably has been little used since. Enoch was a prophet who foretold the outpouring of judgment on the earth (Jude 14-15), and the arrival of his son deepened his convictions. Doctor Lang states the meaning of the name was *"It shall not come till he die."* It can hardly be a coincidence that, from the names and years mentioned in the fifth chapter of Genesis, the devastating flood of Noah's day began in the year that Methuselah died. The man lived 969 years and some of his contemporaries surely thought he would never die. The length of the patriarch's life was an indication of the mercy of God. Judgment would coincide with the death of Methuselah, and therefore, the longer he lived the greater became the opportunity for sinners to repent.

Abraham . . . the delay to prove God's man! (Gen. 22:16-18)

The birth of Isaac was a miracle, for Sarah his mother was beyond the age for childbearing and was barren and incapable of conception. When God announced she would bear a son, it seemed ridiculous, and the woman became convulsed with laughter. (See Gen. 18:12.) Yet, the miracle happened, and no language could describe the joy of Abraham when he beheld the impossible! God promised that in Isaac should all people be blessed, that his seed would be as the sand upon the seashore. It was surprising when Abraham was asked to sacrifice his boy upon an altar. The patriarch was a seer who became God's friend. He considered the matter and came to a conclusion. If Isaac died *and remained dead,* he could never have children, and God's promise would never be fulfilled. That realization enabled him to say to his servants, "I and the lad will go yonder and worship, *and come again to you.*" "By faith Abraham, when he was tried, offered up Isaac. . . . Accounting that God was able to raise him up, even from the dead" (Heb. 11:17-19). Yet God delayed rescuing the helpless lad until the last moment, when "Abraham stretched forth his hand, and took the knife to slay his son." However great the man's faith, the prospect of plunging a dagger into the heart of his beloved son was frightening. God watched with interest as the saint triumphed and then said, "Because thou hast done this thing . . . in blessing I will bless thee."

Hannah . . . The delay to produce God's messenger (1 Sam. 1:11)

A dedicated woman can be a joy to the soul; a nagging one is a pain in the neck! Elkanah, who had two wives, hardly knew what to do to preserve peace in his home. Hannah, the favorite wife, was childless; and, realizing this fact, Penninah taunted, nagged, and probably made Hannah furious. Repeatedly she asked God to give her a son, and each time her request was denied. Ultimately, becoming very desperate, the distraught woman "Prayed unto the LORD, and wept sore. And she vowed a vow, and said, O LORD of hosts, if thou wilt . . . give unto thine handmaid a man child, then I will give him unto the LORD all the days of his life" (1 Sam. 1:11). Then God smiled and said, "At last!" Hannah desired a son to prevent the nagging of her rival; God looked for a man to save a nation from destruction. When Hannah exhibited total surrender, her prayer was granted instantly. The Lord was very wise. He waited a long time before granting the request of that desperate woman.

Mary of Bethany . . . the delay to perfect his method (John 11:6)

"When [Jesus] had heard therefore that [Lazarus] was sick, he abode two days still in the same place where he was." Probably this was one of the strangest delays of all time! It was difficult for Mary to believe the Savior would not respond to her request for assistance. He had visited their home, had been given the best they could offer, and for Him to refuse to respond to a cry for help was inconceivable. Yet Jesus, having heard of the situation in Bethany, "*stayed two days* still in the same place where he was." Doubtless, He later explained this was done deliberately. They believed Him to be a friend, preacher, counselor, and possibly the Messiah, but when Martha was questioned on the highway, she said, "Yea, Lord: I believe that thou art the Christ, the Son of God, which should come into the world" (John 11:27). That was her first genuine confession of faith. The Lord had tried to develop that kind of trust for a long time. Finally the sisters recognized Him to be Lord of life and death.

FOUR UNWORTHY MEN . . . and a glorious sequel

Someone said, "Until a man reaches rockbottom, he has no chance of reaching the Rock of Ages." There is reason to believe that this statement reaches the ultimate in wisdom. When a man believes in and proclaims his importance, his virtue may be suspect. Yet when a man believes he is totally inadequate, it is often possible to find possibilities of true worth amid his failures. A Pharisee prayed in the temple, and, in spite of his eloquent utterances, he lacked true goodness. A publican was overwhelmed by shame, and yet Jesus saw in him the beginning of real accomplishment. The Bible presents at least four shining examples of this type of man.

The schemer . . . Jacob (Gen. 32:10)

Jacob was a cheat, a schemer, a swindler! He stole his brother's birthright and for a time outwitted his father-in-law. All through his strange and bewildering life, Jacob lived by his wits. What he desired, he obtained, even if his methods were ruthless. It was nevertheless a fact of life that sooner or later such a man would meet a greater swindler. The account of Jacob's sojourn in a foreign land and of his dispute regarding two marriages and an inheritance, makes exciting reading. Jacob became homesick for his country and, relying upon his wits, tried to bribe his angry brother. When all failed, the schemer reached rock bottom and said, "I am not worthy" (Gen. 32:10).

The saint . . . John the Baptist (John 1:27)

When John commenced his preaching, he said, "I baptize with water: but there standeth one among you, whom ye know not. He it is, who coming after me is preferred before me, whose shoe's latchet *I am not worthy* to unloose." When we consider how Jesus said of John: "Among those that are born of women there is not a greater prophet than John the Baptist . . . " (Luke 7:28), it appears strange that John should consider himself to be unworthy. Yet the evangelist was comparing himself with Jesus and not with people. There are men who might consider themselves to be very tall if they stood alongside midgets. Yet they would be insignificant if compared with a giant. Even the apostle to the Gentiles said he was the chief of sinners. (See 1 Tim. 1:15.) The best of men, standing before God and their consciences, can only exclaim, "Woe is me! for I am undone; because I am a man of unclean lips . . . " (Isa. 6:5). To reach the Rock of Ages, people must first reach rock bottom!

The soldier . . . the centurion (Luke 7:6)

When Jesus was about to enter the home of the Roman centurion, the soldier became worried and said, " . . . *I am not worthy* that thou shouldest enter under my roof." Many of the people standing there could have argued against that opinion. The Roman was probably the most commendable man in the city. His superiors obviously thought him worthy of promotion; they had made him a captain. The Jews admired his worth, for he had built a synagogue. To do this he must have been a wealthy man and therefore would have been considered worthy of anything! His love for a slave child indicated he was no ordinary soldier; slaves were very cheap in the market place. Yet, he loved that boy and did all he could to save the young life. Everybody considered him to be worthy, including Christ, who said the man's faith exceeded anything found in Israel.

The son . . . the prodigal (Luke 15:21)

This prodigal son sacrificed everything in the hope of discovering happiness in a distant land. Alas, his ambitions were never realized and he finished by stealing food from swine. Only severe anguish brought him to his own personal rock bottom, where his soul yearned to regain what had been lost. When he returned home, he discovered his father had been watching for his return ever since he went away. As the old man's arms encircled the son's shoulders, the prodigal knew he had reached his Rock of Ages. The tears falling from the father's eyes revealed the overflowing compassion in his heart. God is like that!

The best of men, whether they realize it or not, are completely unworthy of God's attention, and, without the glorious sequel, the future would be bleak! John, describing the wonders of heaven, spoke of the Savior and went on to say ten thousand times ten thousand and thousands of thousands will, one day, unite to say, "THOU ART WORTHY." The righteousness of the Lord Jesus will overshadow our blemishes; His beauty will hide our insufficiencies. Without Jesus, the best of people will be bankrupt, both here and in eternity.

MOSES . . . who had much in common with Isaiah and Paul (EXODUS 3:1-10; ISAIAH 6:1-9; ACTS 22:6-21)

The text "I saw the Lord" is unique; it fits into the life style of every biblical saint, but three men stand out in bold relief. For the purpose of this study we shall discuss two propositions.

No man can see God and not have an urge to serve Him

Moses was leading his flock in the desert when suddenly he saw a burning bush. When he approached the phenomenon, he discovered God was present; the resplendent glory of the Highest had transformed a common shrub into a temporary habitation for the Lord. When God spoke about the necessity of delivering His people from bondage in Egypt and commissioned His servant to be the appointed rescuer, Moses replied he was unable to do the job. Finally, he was bluntly told to do what had been commanded.

Isaiah was praying at the bedside of his royal friend; but his sincere requests were not granted, and eventually the king died. Later he wrote: "In the year that king Uzziah died I saw also the Lord. . . . And he said, Go and tell this people, Hear ye indeed, but understand not; and see ye indeed, but perceive not" (Isa. 6:1-9). The people to whom Isaiah was sent were wicked and cruel; they rejected and stoned God's messengers. It was not easy for Isaiah to preach to people who were "stiff-necked and hardened in heart," but his vision of God led to an irresistible call to service.

The greatest desire ever to fill the heart of Paul was the prospect of winning his Jewish friends. He reasoned that, if any person could influence the nation, he could. They knew him; he had received letters from the high priest. If the Jews would listen to anybody, they would listen to him! Acts 22:21 relates how the Lord interrupted Paul's arguments by saying: "Depart: for I will send thee far hence unto the Gentiles." Whenever Paul encountered persecution, it was the result of his going to the synagogue. Had he been more concerned about Gentiles, he would have avoided most of his trouble. He never lost his desire to win Israel and much later in life wrote: "I say the truth in Christ, I lie not . . . I have great heaviness and continual sorrow in my heart. For I could wish that myself were accursed from Christ for my brethren, my kinsmen according to the flesh" (Rom. 9:1-3). All three of the men mentioned saw the Lord and could not escape the call to service.

No man dare serve until he has seen the Lord — the task is too difficult!

Moses gave his life to help the most undeserving people in the world. Even in the wilderness they said they would have preferred to stay in Egypt, where there was plenty of ground in which to be buried. Isaiah preached to rebellious people who were accustomed to stoning prophets. Their insults were continuous; their mockery was unforgiveable. Yet it was incumbent on God and His servant to do what could be done to warn the decadent nation. Unless Isaiah had often communicated with his God, he would have been unable to exercise his ministry.

Paul at the end of his life was almost alone; most of his helpers had forsaken him. Some irresponsible converts exhibited shallowness of Christian experience when they compared Paul with Peter and Apollos. They grieved the man who led them to Christ. Even Paul became discouraged, and it was necessary for God to speak comforting, reassuring words to His servant when the apostle was imprisoned in Jerusalem. The study of these scriptures proves that working for God is often a hazardous affair; no person should expect an easy time following Christ. To SEE GOD is to receive a call to serve; to labor without that vision leads to failure, disappointment, and despair.

If these two propositions be correct, it becomes interesting to ask why so many people within the churches have no desire to serve the Lord. They are content to attend services, place an offering on the collection plate, greet other members, but have no burden to serve and no enthusiasm for the extension of Christ's kingdom. Have they ever seen the Lord? The failure of many Christian workers suggests that, even if they saw God, they did not see Him often enough. What should have been a privilege and a delight became an intolerable burden, a drudgery, and a nightmare. Many who put their hands to the plough turned back and became unworthy of God's kingdom. Our fore-fathers died to preserve the faith, but some of their descendants faint at the sight of one spot of blood!

THREE MIDNIGHTS . . . and the cries in the dark

Midnight is not an ideal time to welcome visitors! It is hardly the opportune moment to entertain friends. Apart from the people who either prepare for the next day or whose job concerns the protection of others, midnight is the time when the world slumbers. A day with its opportunities has gone; the next with its possibilities has not yet arrived, and in between, for better or for worse, men sleep. Maybe this explains why, in Bible times, many things happened at midnight.

The midnight cry of grief (Exod. 12:29-30)

Pharaoh had been told repeatedly of approaching disaster, but persistently he ignored the warnings of Moses. He refused to liberate his slaves and in defiance of God's commands deliberately increased their burdens. Men emulating this example can only blame themselves when disaster arrives. It was at that time God instituted the Passover, and two things stand out in bold relief. The first was a change in the calendar! We have no way of knowing at what time of the year or what week of the month all the events took place; we only know that God abruptly changed the calendar and commanded His people to begin a new year. The second concerned the manner in which the Hebrews celebrated the feast. "And thus shall ye eat it; with your loins girded, your shoes on your feet, and your staff in your hand; and ye shall eat it in haste: it is the Lord's passover" (Exod. 12:11). Obviously the participants were to be ready to leave immediately. The midnight hour was about to strike, and the Hebrews were expected to walk by faith into a new life. It was the beginning of a new year! Soon cries of anguish would re-echo throughout Egypt, for the judgment of God was about to slay the firstborn of every family. The Egyptians had wasted their final opportunity to gain favor with God; their belated repentance would be too late to prevent a catastrophe. When Pharaoh and his legions died in the surging waters of the Red Sea, evidence was supplied that God meant what He said.

The midnight cry of gratitude (Acts 16:25)

The prison at Philippi was very dark and silent. Most of the inmates were either asleep or trying to sleep. The guards were at ease, but for two men slumber was elusive. The day had been eventful, for a crowd had tried to murder them. The aching backs of the prisoners bore eloquent testimony to the pain inflicted by lashing whips. Paul and Silas had delivered a demon-possessed girl and by so doing had enraged the despicable men who used her to increase their riches. Infuriated because their dupe had escaped, the citizens dragged the preachers to the town square, where a riot had been incited. The shouting and accusations were still ringing in the minds of the preachers, and every movement of their bodies reminded them of the merciless thrashing that had lacerated their backs. Most men would have questioned the wisdom and kindness of God. Why had He permitted this to happen to His faithful servants? Perhaps it was then that Paul whispered to Silas, "Let's sing." "And at midnight Paul and Silas prayed, and sang praises unto God: and the prisoners heard them." When God heard the songs of His servants, He summoned the forces of nature to provide an accompaniment for their praise. "And suddenly there was a great earthquake, so that the foundations of the prison were shaken: and immediately all the doors were opened, and every one's bands were loosed" (v. 26). Did the other inmates of the prison curse, shout, complain, or marvel? Probably they had never heard singing at midnight, unless one of their companions somehow had obtained enough liquor to get drunk! There had to be a reason why men in pain could sing in the dark! There was; they were not alone; the risen Christ was with them and His grace was sufficient!

The midnight cry of gladness (Matt. 25:6)

"And at midnight there was a cry made, Behold, the bridegroom cometh; go ye out to meet him." This parable of Jesus was easily understood by listeners, for such scenes were commonplace in Israel. It was customary for friends of the bridegroom to meet and accompany him to the place where the ceremony would take place. If the bridegroom came from a distance, often it was necessary to meet him at night, and then the welcoming party carried lanterns. Sometimes, when the exact hour of arrival was unknown, the friends would sleep, but they were always waiting to hear the cry, "Behold, the bridegroom cometh."

Jesus deliberately took a commonplace incident and clothed it with eternal truth. Someday He would be married! He would woo and win His bride and then come from His Father's home to claim His beloved — the church. Constantly he emphasized that no one knew the precise moment when this would take place but stressed the fact that His followers should remain ready. Conditions would deteriorate in the world, and darkness would prevail among nations. His disciples should never despair. Nation would rise against nation, and unfortunately, many saints would suffer and die for their faith. Great would be their reward. The others who remained were to be faithful and watching, for in such an hour as they thought not the Son of man would come. Then suffering would be overshadowed by the marriage of the Lamb; the hardships encountered along the road of life would be forgotten when the bride met the divine Bridegroom to remain with Him eternally.

MOSES AND JEHU . . . who asked vital questions

(EXODUS 32:26; 2 KINGS 9:32)

Moses, apparently, had been away too long! When the shepherd stayed forty days and nights in the mountain, his human sheep wandered into sin. Aaron, unfortunately, was too weak to prevent the decadence and, yielding to the demands of the majority, accepted gifts and made a golden calf. This had been erected within the camp and, the hilarious, arrogant people arranged an idolatrous carnival inside the sacred compound. "Then Moses stood in the gate of the camp, and said, Who is on the LORD'S side? let him come unto me." (Exod. 32:26).

Jehu had been anointed king, and the Spirit of the Lord rested on him. Jehu was approaching the city of Jezreel, and fear filled the hearts of many citizens. The former king, who had not been dethroned, sent messengers to ascertain whether or not Jehu came peacefully, but the men joined the approaching army and did not return. Later, when Jehu rode triumphantly into the city, "Jezebel . . . painted her face, and tired her head, and looked out at a window. And as Jehu entered in at the gate, she said, Had Zimri peace, who slew his master? And he lifted up his face to the window, and said, Who is on my side? who? And there looked out to him two or three eunuchs. And he said, Throw her down. So they threw her down: and some of her blood was sprinkled on the wall, and on the horses: and he trode her underfoot" (2 Kings 9:30-33).

These two incidents suggest certain propositions.

PROPOSITION 1. *There comes a time when a person needs to know what he believes.*

Involvement in anything is something avidly shunned by many indecisive people. They resemble weather cocks that sit on the top of church steeples; they change direction repeatedly. Swayed by the winds of circumstance, these folk specialize in constantly adjusting and have nothing of permanent value. This may appear to be advantageous, but in matters of eternal realities it is deadly. The Lord said, "He that is not with me is against me" (Matt. 12:30). There is no half-way position. Many procrastinators dislike the alternative of black or white; they prefer to live in a gray area, uncommitted to any course of action. It remains indisputable that in matters of life and death, neutrality is not advisable; what is believed may decide eternal destiny.

PROPOSITION 2. *There comes a time when a person needs to confess what he believes.*

When Moses descended from the Mount of God, he saw within the camp of Israel abominable conditions, and his question, "Who is on the LORD'S side?" made it perfectly clear there could be no secret believers. There might have been many people who secretly admired Moses, who believed in the integrity of their leader. Yet, so it would seem, only the Levites responded to the challenge and went forth to stand beside God's servant. They exhibited courage with their conviction. Later, when Jehu looked up at the painted face of Jezebel, his cry asked if there was any within the house who hated the sinful regime of the nation, whose affiliation was with the new captain whom God had appointed to be king. Not to show one's face at the window would have been evidence the people were either afraid or were supportive of the terrible woman who had brought sorrow and sin to the nation. There have always been occasions when men needed to stand up and be counted! This immortal precept was also true in regard to the personality and claims of Jesus.

PROPOSITION 3. *There comes a time when a person must act against evil.*

It is not enough to agree with virtue; it is necessary to resist evil. The eunuchs who looked down from the windows made a decision. They had to be supportive of either Jehu or Jezebel; it was impossible to be friends of both. When Moses angrily looked upon the people worshiping the golden calf, it became obvious that judgment was about to destroy them. They had forgotten the deliverance from Egypt and, ignoring the claims of Jehovah, degraded themselves and dishonored God. The men who responded to Moses' call, were required to take their swords and become instruments of divine vengeance. (See Exod. 32:27-28.) Someone has said, "If you do not stand for something, you will fall for anything." Within the ranks of *dedicated* Christians there is no paralysis of the soul.

PROPOSITION 4. *What a person does on earth is remembered in eternity.*

Moses was a tremendous leader who carried the guilt and burdens of his people upon his heart. Returning to the mountain, he said to God, "Oh, this people have sinned a great sin . . . . Yet now, if thou wilt forgive their sin—; and if not, blot me, I pray thee, out of thy book which thou hast written. And the LORD said unto Moses, Whosoever hath sinned against me, him will I blot out of my book" (Exod. 32:31-33). It is evident that records are kept in heaven, and in those volumes are written the names of God's people. That God would say He would erase names from the book suggests the possibility of their being eternally lost. Under law, salvation largely depended upon personal righteousness, and people who were unrepentent reached a point of no return where pardon became an impossibility. (See also Rev. 20:12,15.) Broken vows are poor lifebelts in eternal storms.

MOSES . . . who was insistent about two commandments (LEVITICUS 6:12-13; EXODUS 27:20)

The camp of Israel pitched their tents around the tabernacle, which was the center of every facet of Hebrew life. Within the precincts of that consecrated building stood the great altar upon which fire burned. This same order applied within the two temples that succeeded the tabernacle in the history of the Jewish people. However, it becomes thought-provoking when the measurements of the respective altars are compared. The great altar erected by Moses was eight feet square by five feet high. The altar in Solomon's temple was larger, measuring thirty-five feet square by seventeen feet high. When Herod built his magnificent sanctuary, the altar was eighty feet square by twenty-five feet high. These figures suggest the nation had made great progress; nevertheless, with the passing of centuries, there was more altar than fire!

Fire descending

When the altar was first made, the fire came down from heaven. Afterward it became the duty of the priests to maintain what God had commenced. This created within Israel a new industry. Men felled trees in the mountains; others cut them into sizable logs; others transported the timber to the tabernacle and stacked it in convenient places.

Fire demanding

Whenever the fire needed additional fuel, the officials knew where to obtain supplies, and thus day after day the flames burned upon the altar of Jehovah. It was unfortunate that, prior to the appearance of Samuel, the commandments had been forgotten or ignored, and the fire went out.

Fire dying

It would appear that the priests became indolent; they neglected their God-given tasks and gave more attention to matters of lesser importance. Apathy spread through the nation, prophets were stoned and beaten, and the fall of the nation was assured. All these details are important, for they remind us of the fire that should be burning on the altar of *our* inmost being. If the glow of spirituality is to radiate from our souls, we must feed the fires kindled at conversion, and by constant attention be assured the warmth of true godliness will never diminish. Jesus warned His disciples saying, "And because iniquity shall abound, the love of many shall wax cold" (Matt. 24:12). It behooves every Christian to keep the fires of consecration burning brightly.

The second outstanding commandment given by Moses concerned the lamp within the sanctuary. Moses said, "And thou shalt command the children of Israel, that they bring thee pure oil olive beaten for the light, to cause the lamp to burn always" (Exod. 27:20). It was a cause for regret that this commandment was ultimately forgotten. "And ere the lamp of God went out in the temple of the LORD, where the ark of God was, and Samuel was laid down to sleep; That the LORD called Samuel: and he answered, Here am I" (1 Sam. 3:3-4). Zechariah supplies a great example of the safest method of assuring the continuance of this ministry. "What seest thou? And I said, I have looked, and behold a candlestick [lampstand] all of gold, with a bowl upon the top of it, and his seven lamps thereon, and seven pipes to the seven lamps, which are upon the top thereof. And two olive trees by it, one upon the right side of the bowl, and the other upon the left side thereof" (Zech. 4:2-3). The bowls fed oil into the lamps, and thus the light was maintained. Obviously the pipes had to be free of hindrances preventing the flow of oil, otherwise the lamps would cease to shine. The entire picture suggests (1) A shining light; (2) A sustained light; (3) A stifled or starved light.

It should be emphasized that the Old Testament commandments relate to us. First, the fires consume the sacrifice, then the light shines into the surrounding darkness. Everything of self should be placed upon God's altar; every particle of dross should be destroyed. Then our lives become a sacrifice wholy acceptable unto the Lord. Paul wrote: "I beseech you therefore, brethren, by the mercies of God, that ye present your bodies a living sacrifice, holy, acceptable unto God, which is your reasonable service" (Rom. 12:1). The fires of sacrificial devotion should never go out, and the same is true of our testimony. The Holy Spirit, the oil of God's sufficiency, only flows through clean, open channels. If these are maintained in our lives, then the light of a radiant testimony will never be extinguished. Jesus said, "Let your light so shine before men, that they may see your good works, and glorify your Father which is in heaven" (Matt. 5:16).

FOUR LITTLE DONKEYS . . . and what they said (EXODUS 34:20; NUMBERS 22:28; MARK 11:2; JUDGES 15:15)

I once shocked my Sunday morning congregation by calling them "a group of donkeys." My remarks were not appreciated until I smiled and admitted it was the greatest compliment I could give. In the Western world, a donkey is the strange animal with the raucus cry and big ears. Yet in the Middle East, a donkey is the most precious asset of every peasant. The man kicks his chicken and his dog. He will certainly shout at his wife, but he loves his donkey. I have seen these little animals heavily laden with produce, trotting off to the market. I have watched as they returned with empty baskets piled high on either side of their backs. When there is neither produce nor baskets, I have watched as the peasant, riding like a king, proudly returned to his mud-brick palace in the fields. He always rides his little donkey, while the wife walks behind carrying packages. The donkey is a very precious animal, has a very special place within the Bible.

The delivered donkey . . . serving (Exod. 34:20)

The children of Israel had strict dietary laws that were faithfully observed. Some animals were considered to be unclean, and among these was the donkey. Even from the moment of birth, it was condemned. Children might fondle it, and its owner might desire it, but the law was unyielding. "But the firstling of an ass thou shalt redeem with a lamb: and if thou redeem him not, then shalt thou break his neck" (Exod. 34:20). Through no fault of its own, the little animal was condemned. If we may use words that describe sinners, then "it was born in sin and shapen in iniquity." It could only live because someone loved it sufficiently to redeem it. Thus did God try to teach His people the message of the gospel. Unrelenting law condemns us by saying: "The soul that sinneth must die" (Ezek. 18:20). Condemnation and death would be inescapable but for the fact that God supplied a Lamb for our redemption. If it were possible to ask a donkey working hard in the fields, "Why do you work so hard?," its reply would be instantaneous: "I have been redeemed; this is the least I can do for my Master."

The disturbed donkey . . . speaking (Num. 22:28)

The children of Israel were marching through the wilderness to Canaan, and their continuing success terrorized their enemies. A king named Balak was so frightened he invited a diviner called Balaam to curse the Hebrews. When the invitation was refused, the monarch tried to bribe the strange prophet, and so great was the reward offered that the pseudo-prophet found it difficult to reject the chance to become wealthy. He saddled his ass and went on his mission, and it soon became evident the donkey had more brains and keener eyesight than his master. The prophet was pursuing a path to destruction, and the only thing that stood between him and disaster was the ass upon which he rode. The donkey's testimony saved Balaam's life. It should remind all who have been redeemed they should be willing to witness a good confession.

The difficult donkey . . . surrendering (Mark 11:2)

"Ye shall find a colt tied, whereon never man sat; loose him, and bring him." It is significant to remember that Matthew's gospel (21:2) says the young donkey was with its mother; therefore the danger was twofold. The men would have to cope with the older donkey, whose offspring was apparently being stolen. Since the young donkey had never been tamed, all its fiery disposition would be challenged by the human intruders. It was amazing how the colt patiently submitted to the claims of Jesus. There is reason to believe that the donkey proudly carried the Savior down the street and was determined to remain reliable even to the end of the journey. Never for a moment did the Lord have any anxiety; His young steed was completely reliable. It would be wonderful if every Christian were as faithful as that little animal.

The dead donkey . . . slaying (Judg. 15:15)

This incident belongs to the darkest days in Israel's history. The Philistines had persecuted Israel for twenty years, but then came Samson! He was God's man for that generation. One day, when enemies were taunting him, he looked around for a weapon and saw the jawbone of an ass. We know nothing about the donkey except that it had died, and that in death it became more powerful than it ever had been in life. The fact that it is recorded the jawbone was "moist" seems to indicate the animal had only recently died; there had been insufficient time for the sun to dry it out. Samson lifted the jawbone and with it slew a thousand Philistines. That bone would not have been available had the animal been alive. Here there may be veiled foreshadowings of the New Testament truth that teaches Christians can only be of maximum use for Christ when they have become selfless. Paul said, "I am crucified with Christ: nevertheless I live; yet not I, but Christ liveth in me: and the life which I now live in the flesh I live by the faith of the Son of God, who loved me, and gave himself for me" (Gal. 2:20). The story of Pentecost tells how God took a donkey of another type to defeat the purposes of evil. Simon Peter, who had denied his Lord at the fire, had learned how to die to self, and it was only then that God could take "his jawbone" to do the impossible. Don't be upset if you are ever called "a donkey." Rejoice! You had wonderful ancestors!

MOSES . . . who supplied a sermon for Christ

(NUMBERS 21:9; JOHN 3:14)

The Bible is a library of sixty-six books, but each is inextricably woven into the fabric of the whole. The Old Testament is a prediction of the New Testament, which naturally became the fulfillment of earlier statements. There is reason to believe that Jesus was the greatest student ever to study the Old Testament prophets, and almost every day He repeated the statements of ancient authors. When the Lord spoke with Nicodemus, He mentioned an incident from the writings of Moses, and what He said has inspired innumerable sermons.

The stricken people

The children of Israel were in serious trouble; their inexcusable criticism and complaints had angered the Almighty, and judgment had fallen upon many people. Fiery serpents appeared from every direction to bite or sting the offenders, and the sufferings of the tribes beggared description. The serpents came from under rocks, from holes in the ground, from bushes, from everywhere. They slid into tents, hid in clothing and under beds; they represented the greatest menace Israel had ever known. The venom of the serpents was killing many thousands of people. Ultimately, the realization of need drove the people to their knees; and, when that happened, there was hope for dying sinners.

A sincere prayer

Feeling too unworthy to pray for themselves, they besought Moses saying, "We have sinned . . . pray unto the LORD, that he take away the serpents from us. And Moses prayed for the people" (Num. 21:7-8). The answers to some prayers are often delayed, but the sincere request for forgiveness is granted immediately. When prodigals return, they are instantly welcomed by the outstretched arms of God's eternal love. The Bible supplies innumerable examples of this amazing truth. God's kindness always exceeds man's sin.

A serpent's pole

"And the LORD said unto Moses, Make thee a fiery serpent, and set it upon a pole: and it shall come to pass, that every one that is bitten, when he looketh upon it, shall live" (Num. 21:8). The venom of the serpent can only represent the poison of sin which comes from "that old serpent the devil." The *brazen serpent* therefore indicates that he who caused the trouble would himself be defeated when a pole was lifted high. God promised Moses that when a sinner looked at what had been supplied his action would bring salvation. When the people did as they were instructed, God honored His promise so that healing began to reach the homes of the nation. An old hymn could easily have become the national message: "Look and live, my brother, live."

A superb promise

The scene that followed the proclamation made by Moses was electrifying. Dying people were miraculously healed; groans of pain were replaced by shouts of joy. The results were compounded when healed people ran through the camp lifting friends, that they also could see the brazen serpent. Possibly they remained unaware of the implications of that great event. Those miraculous events represented the greatest revival in Israel's history. Healing was not found in any conformity to Mosaic laws, it did not rest upon the rite of circumcision, and it had nothing to do with social status. Everybody was in danger; every one was urged to "look and live;" all who did were not disappointed.

A sublime pattern

It must have been a thrilling experience for Nicodemus when the Lord expounded the ancient story. The old serpent would be defeated at Calvary's cross, the venom of sin would be neutralized by the precious blood of Jesus, and hope would be extended to all people. It was necessary for Moses, the great leader of Israel, to explain these facts to his people; it was also necessary for the Lord to reiterate the same truths to the ruler of the Jews. Likewise, the same responsibility now rests upon the shoulders of all Christians. We have a task to perform, and we must not fail. The eternal destiny of many sinners might be decided by the faithfulness of our ministry.

W. A. Ogden wrote the hymn that became immortalized through the ministry of the great evangelist Ira D. Sankey. The message appears to say all that needs to be said.

> I've a message from the Lord, Hallelujah!
> The message unto you I'll give;
> 'Tis recorded in His Word, Hallelujah!
> It is only that you "look and live."
> I've a message full of love, Hallelujah!
> A message, O my friend, for you;
> 'Tis a message from above, Hallelujah!
> Jesus said it and I know 'tis true.
> Life is offered unto you, Hallelujah!
> Eternal life thy soul shall have,
> If you'll only look to Him, Hallelujah!
> Look to Jesus who alone can save.
> "Look and live," my brother, live,
> Look to Jesus now and live;
> 'Tis recorded in His Word, Hallelujah!
> *It is only that you "look and live."*

THE PEOPLE . . . who built an altar called "Ed"

This is an intriguing story about people who thought they were wiser than God. They admitted His ideas were excellent for other people but not for themselves. During forty years of wandering in the wilderness, Israel had constantly dreamed of the glories of Canaan and had determined not to repeat the mistake made by their ancestors. They rejoiced that the difficulties of the desert would soon be exchanged for the delights of the Promised Land, and the despised manna for the grapes of Eschol.

An attractive possibility (Num. 32:1)

As the time drew near to enter Canaan, some of the people became aware of the attractiveness of the country through which they were traveling; it had excellent pasture suitable for cattle. They began to ask a very potent question: "Why go to Canaan when we can do so much better here?" They had forgotten the sanctuary and thought only of increasing wealth. They ignored the fact that God had called them to a land flowing with milk and honey. The other tribes could live wherever they chose, but they determined to stay where they were and formulate their own life style. They made their decision ignoring the fact they were insulting God, believing their ideas were better than His. Unfortunately, that example has been emulated many times during the history of the church. Many people recognize the beauty of the sanctuary but prefer to stay where assets have a better chance to increase.

An acknowledged problem (Num. 32:16-17)

When Moses objected to the proposal and spoke of their responsibility to the remaining tribes, the men compromised and made new suggestions. They would build temporary homes for their families and stockades for the cattle, and they would help their brethren conquer the enemies in Canaan. Afterward, they would return to their inheritance beyond Jordan. They resembled certain professing Christians who contribute generously to the cause of Christ but prefer to reside where the grass is green and the cattle fat! They followed the pattern set by Lot, who turned his back on the everlasting hills in order to live in Sodom.

An assuming pride (Josh. 22:10)

The battles were over; the land had been subdued. "Then Joshua called the Reubenites, and the Gadites, and the half tribe of Manasseh. . . . and blessed them, and sent them away" (Josh. 22:1-6). The people turned their backs on the tabernacle, the altar, and the God-appointed inheritance and went to count their cattle! After they crossed the river, they looked back. They were seeing things from a distance, and their vision was blurred. They desired to remain God's people even though they lived in a foreign land, and this intense desire made them erect a very large altar which they named "Ed." Their action almost precipitated a civil war in Israel. Why should they be known as Hebrews when they lived apart from their brethren? They remind us of people who object when their names are removed from the church roll. They seldom attend a service and are never active in the sanctuary, but it pleases them to know they belong to a church. They are not heathens!

An assured poverty (1 Chron. 5:23-26)

Cattle are a poor substitute for contentment; prosperity is a poor replacement for peace. Those ancient Hebrews had worshiped around the tabernacle; they had seen the pillar of fire at night and the cloud that hovered over the house of God. Doubtless they had been thrilled by the spectacle; their eyes had become moist when they considered the goodness of God. Alas, they were destined to live on memories, and with the passing of time even those grew dim. Their cattle increased, but their happiness diminished. Ultimately, they lost everything and were among the first to be captured by invading Babylonians. David was wise when he said, "I had rather be a doorkeeper in the house of my God, than to dwell in the tents of wickedness" (Ps. 84:10). God had provided lavishly for His people; alas, the two and one half tribes were too short-sighted to appreciate the glory of their inheritance. They were attracted by grass, not grace; by increasing finances, not by inspiring fellowship. Their cousins are still among us!

GOD . . . and more of His inspired delays

It has often been said, "The wheels of God grind slowly, but they grind exceeding small." When necessary, the Lord can move with devastating speed, but often His movements are in contrast to the ways of earth. Men like speed and often make mistakes trying to reach places too quickly! God sometimes moves with planned precision to accomplish what otherwise would be impossible. The delays of God are among the most absorbing studies in the Bible.

Moses . . . the delay to protect God's people (Deut. 34:4)

It has always appeared regrettable that whereas Moses was denied entry into the Promised Land, others who were far less worthy were allowed to enter. Moses made one mistake and lost his blessing, but the rest of the unworthy nation was given the privilege denied their leader. Eventually, the patriarch did get into the land, for Matthew 17:3 describes how he and Elijah spoke with Christ on the Mount of Transfiguration. The event was greatly delayed, *but Moses did get in*! That delay probably taught Israel one of life's most important lessons. Throughout Old Testament ages, Hebrew mothers told their children about the leader who brought them from the land of Egypt, but the end of the story was always the same. "Children, he never entered this land." When the boys and girls asked the reason, the mother gravely replied, "He disobeyed God." Thus did the Lord teach the nation the value of obeying the voice of Jehovah. It was a lesson they urgently needed to learn.

Job . . . the delay to prove God's promises (Job 42:10)

There is reason to believe that Job was never aware of the drama behind the sufferings that devastated his life. He had no idea that God and Satan were watching closely the events taking place. When continuing catastrophes ruined Job's happiness, when boils and carbuncles made life a misery, Job was uninformed that these were being permitted because the Almighty was intensely proud of His servant. "And the LORD said unto Satan, Hast thou considered my servant Job, that there is none like him in the earth, a perfect and an upright man, one that feareth God, and escheweth evil? Then Satan answered the LORD, and said, Doth Job fear God for nought? Hast not thou made an hedge about him. . . . But put forth thine hand now, and touch all that he hath, and he will curse thee to thy face" (Job 1:8-11). God was intensely proud of Job, but His pride had to be vindicated before the forces of evil. Job had no way of knowing his problems had more repercussions in heaven than on earth. The confidence of God was being challenged. When the conflict terminated, the Lord rewarded Job beyond his wildest dreams. It took time, but the end was never in doubt.

Saul . . . the delay to present God's plan (1 Sam. 13:8-10)

Poor Saul, he was in terrible trouble, and yet he alone was responsible for his dilemma. He had attacked the armies of the Philistines and aroused the anger of Israel's fiercest enemies. They retaliated with "thirty thousand chariots, and six thousand horsemen, and people as the sand which is on the sea shore in multitude" (v. 5). Terror seized the hearts of Saul's soldiers, and desertions were constantly weakening his forces. He expected Samuel to arrive and bless his efforts, but the prophet did not come. "And Saul said, Bring hither a burnt offering to me, and peace offerings. And he offered the burnt offering. And . . . behold, Samuel came . . . . and said, What hast thou done?" Poor Saul, if only he had depended upon God and not on himself. It was illegal for any layman to offer sacrifice, yet Saul took the law into his own hand and sinned. Stupidly he revealed himself unworthy to be the king of God's people and demonstrated what Samuel had known from the beginning. Saul was an irresponsible man whose self confidence destroyed his dependence on God. As the modern expression says, "He had gotten too big for his breeches" and had to make way for a shepherd boy called David. Sometimes God's delays are planned to test us. Blessed is the man in whom God is not disappointed.

Trophimus . . . the delay to protect God's preacher (2 Tim. 4:20)

The power of God to heal the sick had not diminished. Wherever Paul preached the gospel, sick people were helped; sometimes he even touched handkerchiefs that supernaturally conveyed healing. Nevertheless, it should be remembered that Luke, the beloved physician, also shared Paul's ministry. Those who were not healed immediately by Paul became Luke's patients. The doctor did gradually what Paul was unable to do immediately. When enthusiastic faith healers *demand* healing for anybody at any time, they exhibit unscriptural stupidity. Doubtless Paul often became weary and consequently valued all the help available. When Trophimus became sick, one would have thought the apostle's touch would have restored health to the valued assistant. Paul could have prayed all night, but it would have made no difference. When God said "No," Paul could not change God's mind! Trophimus needed a rest, and the Lord deliberately put him on his back! This is a lesson that many preachers need to learn. We are not robots, but human beings who have become temples of the Holy Spirit. To ruin our health by unwise activities is dishonoring to God. It is necessary to recognize that the starts, steps, and stops of a saint should be ordered by the Lord. Sometimes delays in answers to prayers are an indication that God is wiser than His people.

DAVID . . . who knew how to kill giants!

Dear David:

You killed a giant, and we would like to know how you did it. If it were possible to get you on a telephone, we would reserve the line for a day. There is much we wish to know; we are persuaded there was much more to your triumph than the mere slinging of a pebble! Every day, giants of one kind or another threaten us, but unfortunately our sling shots miss their targets. Our Goliath remains, and this is extremely annoying. David, be patient; we are going to imagine you are listening.

You were called (1 Sam. 16:11-13)

David, we have often read the words: "And Samuel said unto Jesse, Are here all thy children? And he said, There remaineth yet the youngest, and, behold, he keepeth the sheep. And Samuel said unto Jesse, Send and fetch him. . . . And he sent, and brought him in. Now he was ruddy, and withal of a beautiful countenance, and goodly to look to. And the LORD said, Arise, anoint him: for this is he." David, pardon our directness, but you were nothing! We can understand why the prophet looked with favor on your eldest brother and momentarily believed he would make an ideal king for Israel. You had nothing to offer but a clean heart, pure motives, and an unfailing trust in God. Maybe that was the reason why God chose you in the first place. Since you were obviously inadequate for what lay ahead, no flesh could glory in God's presence. Perhaps we need to recognize this as basic training for those who would slay giants!

You were concerned (1 Sam. 17:34-35)

When a lion and a bear attacked your animals, you went to their rescue, not knowing God was watching your actions. At that time you had no thought of becoming a great leader in Israel. You were content to do little things, and your faithfulness led to promotion. How often did you practice that sling shot? You probably slung many thousands of pebbles until your aim was perfect. It was not a chance shot that gave Goliath a headache! You practiced incessantly when there were no audience to applaud, and your efforts were rewarded on the field of battle. You graduated slowly, but effectively, in the school of persistent endeavor.

You were courageous (1 Sam. 17:37)

David, it seems unbelievable that, although you were only a child, you saw God, not the giant. Your brethren looked at the mountain of flesh and trembled; you lifted your eyes to the hills from whence came your aid. Was that the secret of your confidence? Your ideas of combat were sensational, for you rejected Saul's armor and disdained everything others would have welcomed. You went to battle utterly dependent upon God, and your fearlessness probably made angels smile. It is easy to imagine that, as you went to meet the adversary, you sang, "Hallelujah, I'm in good company! The battle is not mine; it is the Lord's." David, now that we think about it, your battle was won before it commenced.

You were careful (1 Sam. 17:40)

It seems significant when we read, "he took his staff in his hand, and chose him five smooth stones out of the brook, and put them in a shepherd's bag which he had, even in a scrip; and his sling was in his hand: and he drew near to the Philistine." Why did you choose five pebbles? Were you being careful? Did you say to yourself, "If I miss the first or second time, I will still have reserve ammunition?" Your enthusiasm did not run away with your brains! You were not so self-confident that your reliance on God was undermined. Were you being careful so that nothing would spoil God's triumph? When we think about the matter, we are constrained to confess this is why so many of our giants remain undefeated! We are so self-assured that, while we are shining our armor, Goliath fires a dart before we are aware of his nearness. Of course, we know you only needed one pebble, but we like the idea of having four extra available. Actually, you could have defeated five Goliaths and while the other people were watching, could have gathered more ammunition.

You were a conqueror (1 Sam. 17:50)

When we read the account of the battle's climax, we do not know whether to stand up and cheer, or sit down and think! "There was no sword in the hand of David. Therefore David ran, and stood upon the Philistine, and took his sword, and drew it out of the sheath thereof, and slew him, and cut off his head therewith." You surely put the finishing touch to that conflict! Really, we are very stupid. We protect and encourage some of the giants who threaten our usefulness for God and refrain from "cutting off their heads!"

You were crowned (2 Sam. 2:4)

David, as we review your life, it seems that for most of the time you were a living example of the text: "No good thing will [God] withhold from them that walk uprightly" (Ps. 84:11). Many giants threatened your spiritual welfare, but by God's grace you conquered them. Perhaps if we follow your example, we also will become "*more than conquerors.*"

THE PROPHET . . . who was killed by a lion

(1 KINGS 13:24)

It is a known fact that lions kill when they are hungry, but once an animal has been caught, the killer summons the pride and the feast begins. Afterward, they retire to a quiet place to sleep. If for no other reason, this story becomes exceedingly interesting. Long ago, a lion killed a man, ignored both the corpse and the victim's donkey, and stood peacefully alongside the dead body. That ass was probably the most fortunate animal in the country.

Called to preach (1 Kings 13:1-2)

Abominable events were taking place in Israel. Jeroboam, ignoring the commandments of God, had erected idols and, taking the place of a priest, was offering incense on an alien altar. The arrival of an unknown prophet who denounced the king's deed angered Jeroboam to such an extent that he shouted, "Lay hold of him." The atmosphere became very tense, as if charged with electricity, when that man fearlessly criticized the monarch; it was possibly the bravest act of his life. Yet the preacher was safe as long as he obeyed his Lord.

Courageous and protected (1 Kings 13:4)

Enraged to the point of madness, Jeroboam withdrew his hand from the altar and, reaching out, tried to seize the offender. The onlookers were horrified when the king's arm suddenly stiffened and became paralyzed. He could neither withdraw nor lower it; it seemed turned to stone. The king's friends were terrified, and that probably explained why the prophet remained unmolested. God never sends out His servants alone. Even before the Savior uttered the words, "Lo, I am with you always," the promise was in operation among God's people. Nevertheless, it is wise to remember that some of God's promises are conditional, and all who claim allegiance to the Lord should be aware of His requests.

Considerate in prayer (1 Kings 13:6)

Paralyzed and helpless, the king asked the prophet to intercede on his behalf, to restore life to the afflicted arm — and the man of God did so. Blessed indeed is the preacher whose prayers are answered quickly and graciously. Some might have desired the affliction to remain as a permanent reminder of the king's stupidity. It has been written, "After this thing Jeroboam returned not from his evil way" (13:33). The king regained sensitivity in his arm but lost it in his head and soul.

Careless in proceeding (1 Kings 13:8-9, 15-19)

The prophet's repetition of the instructions received from God made it clear there was to be no fraternizing with the enemy. It seemed shameful that an old prophet should have become a menace. It was incomprehensible that a preacher could become a liar. It must be remembered that the entire nation was decadent and irresponsible. The greatest need of that generation was discipline which promoted and encouraged obedience to the revealed will of God. Everyone's eyes were focused on that foolish prophet; what happened to him would be described many times in the homes of the nation. The prophet's unfortunate demise can only be understood when viewed from that angle. God permitted the death of a disobedient preacher in an attempt to rescue thousands of precious souls.

Condemned and perishing (1 Kings 13:23-24)

"And it came to pass, after he had eaten bread, and after he had drunk, that he saddled for him the ass, to wit, for the prophet whom he had brought back. And when he was gone, a lion met him by the way, and slew him: and his carcass was cast in the way, and the ass stood by it, and the lion also stood by the carcass." It might be beneficial to compare two incidents. This lion savagely killed a disobedient prophet; yet other lions refused to harm Daniel who also was a servant of God. (See Dan. 6:20-22.) Thus did God endeavor to instruct His wayward people, and thus would He teach us. Lions, and many other enemies, become harmless when the Lord is enthroned in the hearts of His trusting children.

The two preachers described in this strange story provide an illuminating contrast. One was young and enthusiastic; the other was old and untruthful. Was the older man a little jealous because another had been chosen by God to undertake a special mission? We may never know the answer to that question but it behooves every servant of God to keep his soul clean, so that at the end of life's journey, he will be able to say with Paul, "I have fought a good fight, I have finished my course, I have kept the faith: Henceforth there is laid up for me a crown . . ." (2 Tim. 4:7-8).

GOD AND ELIJAH . . . who found each other in a cave

(1 KINGS 19:13)

A fallen giant is the most pathetic sight in the world. I shall always remember speaking with a forest ranger after a terrible storm had swept over North America. Regretfully he said over 200 giant trees had fallen during the night and it would take years to remove them from the mountain. I have seen other giants equally pathetic. I have known a millionaire alcoholic, a clergyman who occupied a prison cell, a famous athlete banished from sports because of continuing indiscretions. The story of Elijah surpasses them all.

A man in the storm . . . God forgotten

High in one of the steep ravines of Mount Horeb was a little cave of shadows. It was very far from the crowded cities and was visited only by birds, mountain animals, and, occasionally, a lonely hunter. It was toward this cave Israel's greatest prophet slowly made his way. He was tired, despondent, and desperately lonely. He believed himself to be Israel's greatest failure, and was aware that by this time the entire nation knew the man of steel had become a man of humiliating weakness. As Elijah tramped toward his destination, he knew his ministry had terminated. If he preached again the people would laugh. Poor man, he was destined to live with himself, and in that frame of mind he was not a good companion! He had been a marvelous warrior for God in the big battles of life but had been defeated by the threat of a sinful queen. He had no idea what to do next and probably could not have cared less.

A man in the shadows . . . God following

"But [Elijah] went a day's journey into the wilderness, and came and sat down under a juniper tree: and he requested for himself that he might die; and said, It is enough; now, O Lord, take away my life; for I am not better than my fathers. And as he lay and slept under a juniper tree, behold . . . an angel . . . " (1 Kings 19:4-5). It is stimulating to know that, although the prophet was out of God's favor, he was never out of His sight. "*Behold . . . an angel.*" When he reached the cave, he probably leaned against the rock and asked, "What do my friends think of me now?" Since that time many fallen giants have asked the same question. When a person is haunted by memories of failure, peace becomes the most elusive thing in the world. During moments of weariness, Elijah had been visited by helpful strangers. Did he recognize them to be God's angels in disguise? If he did, he would have appreciated George Matheson's immortal hymn: "O love that wilt not let me go." Suddenly, he was listening to the voice of God. "What doest thou *here* Elijah?"

His response was instantaneous: "I have been very jealous for the LORD God of hosts . . . and I, even I only, am left; and they seek my life, to take it away" (v. 10). Poor man, he might have said, "O Lord, I have failed You," but pride superceded his wisdom.

A man in the stillness . . . God forgiving

"And [God] said, Go forth, and stand upon the mount before the LORD. And, behold, the LORD passed by, and a great and strong wind rent the mountains . . . but the LORD was not in the wind . . . and after the wind an earthquake; but the LORD was not in the earthquake: and after the earthquake a fire; but the LORD was not in the fire: and after the fire a still small voice [a quiet, gentle whisper] . . . and Elijah . . . wrapped his face in his mantle" (vv. 19:11-13). God had found him, and, as the moments passed, he found God. The Lord's grace always exceeds our sin. It is not possible for any person to run far enough nor fast enough to get away from the Lord. Whatever the destination may be, God is always there to greet us, to heal our wounds, to lead us beside still waters and into green pastures.

It was true that Elijah's ministry ended prematurely, but God graciously honored His servant. Within a short time the Lord supplied a chariot of splendor to take the prophet to the palace of the King of Kings, where doubtless he received a new commission. There is reason to believe that in glory he met Moses for the first time; they had much in common. Both had failed because of little things. The two stalwarts became great friends, and there was no cause for amazement when they were commissioned to minister to Christ on the Mount of Transfiguration. (See Matt. 17:3.) As Dr. Robert Schuller often says, "They turned their scars into stars!" We also shall do well if we look beyond our failures to anticipate greater successes for Christ and His kingdom.

GOD . . . who laughs at impossibilities

Years ago, my friend Dr. Edwin Orr wrote a book entitled *Can God?* The volume encouraged people to believe that nothing was too hard for the Almighty to accomplish. The author published additional books expounding the same truth, but they were all based on the same theme. God laughed at impossibilities, and the greater the problem, the greater the opportunity for Him to display His amazing power. Dr. Orr doubtless derived his inspiration from a thoughtful consideration of God's Word.

Can God furnish a table in the wilderness? . . . the obstinate crowd (Ps. 78:19)

The children of Israel were becoming increasingly restless. They were surrounded by the sands of a desert; food was in short supply; water was at a premium; outspoken condemnation of Moses was being heard everywhere. Long afterward, David, describing the scene, said, "Yea, they spake against God; they said, *Can God furnish a table in the wilderness?*" It has often been claimed that man's extremity is God's opportunity; but, alas, when most men encounter problems, they only invite God to intervene when other possibilities have been exhausted. Unfortunately, the Lord is denied the privilege of helping His children until it is almost impossible to do anything. History proves that even when men confused the issue, the grace of God was sufficient to do the impossible. Throughout the wilderness experiences, God sent manna from heaven and birds to sustain His hungry people. He met their every need, but unfortunately thankfulness was ruined by ingratitude. Complaints and criticisms warped their thinking and turned joy into sadness. Nevertheless, He did furnish a table in the wilderness and still does for all who trust Him.

Can God open a window in heaven? . . . the outspoken critic (2 Kings 7:2)

The city of Samaria was in terrible trouble. The Syrian army had surrounded the walls, and inside, people were starving to death. "And there was a great famine in Samaria; and, behold, they besieged it, until an ass's head was sold for fourscore pieces of silver, and the fourth part of a cab of dove's dung for five pieces of silver" (2 Kings 6:25). One woman boiled her son that she might eat his flesh, but another, who shared the meal, refused to follow her example when the need for additional food became urgent. Then an unbelievable event occurred. The prophet Elisha said, "Hear ye the word of the LORD, tomorrow about this time shall a measure of fine flour be sold for a shekel, and two measures of barley for a shekel in the gate of Samaria" (7:1). *Had the prophet had taken leave of his senses?* "Then a lord on whose hand the king leaned answered the man of God, and said, Behold, if the LORD would make windows in heaven, might this thing be?" Unbelief grasps at straws; faith clings to the promises of God. Read 2 Kings 7 and remember that God can still open windows in heaven--in one way or another!

Can God multiply a little? . . . the ominous conditions (Mark 8:4)

A wilderness was a terrible place in which to have a picnic, especially when there were neither food nor stores within miles. Jesus, perhaps deliberately, had led thousands of people to the solitary place where need had become urgent. The people were very hungry, for they had been with the Lord for three days. With each moment, the problems of hunger were being accentuated. When the Lord asked the disciples to feed the multitude, His suggestion seemed ludicrous. "And his disciples answered him, From whence can a man satisfy these men with bread here in the wilderness?" What happened afterward is now known throughout the world. The Lord graciously accepted a boy's lunch, blessed it, and fed a multitude of hungry people. It is not known whether the boy had been with Jesus for three days. If so, then we are confronted by another miracle. When I was a small child, I went with others camping. My thoughtful mother gave me enough food to last a week, but I ate it all the first day. Somehow, the lad still had a supply, and that provides food for thought! All the Lord requires is that we do our best, and He does the rest!

Can God find an island in a fog? . . . the overruling Christ (Acts 27:26)

The story recorded in Acts 27 is one of the greatest maritime adventures of all time. The graphic details supplied by Luke excite the imagination but chill the soul. He wrote: "And we being exceedingly tossed with a tempest . . . lightened the ship . . . . And when neither sun nor stars in many days appeared, and no small tempest lay on us, all hope that we should be saved was then taken away." But when the crew and passengers were despairing, Paul was praying, and "after long abstinence, Paul stood forth in the midst of them, and said, . . . be of good cheer . . . we must be cast upon a certain island" (vv. 14-26). The Bible records how the men were ultimately cast upon the island of Malta. What would have happened if, somehow, that ship had missed the island? A gentleman acquainted with the Mediterranean Sea somberly answered my question when he said, "Sir, it would have piled up on the shores of North Africa." Although the people on the ship were unaware of the fact, God was the unrecognized Pilot on the storm-tossed vessel. He can see *even in the dark* and always knows where He is going!

THE PROPHETS . . . who believed God's Word would last

(PSALM 119:89; ISAIAH 40:8; MATTHEW 24:35; 1 PETER 1:25)

One of the most thrilling features to be found in the Bible is the confidence ancient writers had in their message. Unlike modern authors, the prophets believed God meant what He said; they had unlimited faith in the message they proclaimed. The psalmist said, "For ever, O LORD, thy word is settled in heaven" (119:89). Isaiah declared "The grass withereth, the flower fadeth: but the word of our God shall stand for ever" (40:8). The Savior said, "Heaven and earth shall pass away, but my words shall not pass away" (Matt. 24:35). Peter wrote: "But the word of the Lord endureth for ever. And this is the word which by the gospel is preached unto you" (1 Peter 1:25). It should be remembered these utterances were made thousands of years ago; we are privileged to live in a much later age and can see how the faith of those ancient preachers was justified. It is now possible to explain why men continue to believe in the written Word of God.

Its miraculous preservation

No other volume can compare with the Bible. It was written by many writers, in several countries, and in at least three languages. It was produced over a period of numerous centuries, and its authors came from several walks in life. Amos was a herdsman; Isaiah was a friend of a king; David was a king; Luke was a medical doctor; Paul was a tentmaker; Matthew, a taxgatherer; and several were ordinary fishermen. These men lived at different times, often centuries apart, and yet in some mysterious fashion their works harmonized, their predictions centering on one Man. They were ridiculed and often beaten; their writings were destroyed by fire. (See Jer. 36:22-23.) Printing presses were unknown in ancient times, and therefore all copies of the Scripture had to be written by hand. This was a laborious task, and replacement of worn or destroyed copies was not easy. The custodians of those scrolls were captives in Babylon for seventy years, but their priceless records were preserved. Repeatedly their city was sacked by invading armies; the temple was desecrated and ultimately destroyed. Though most of Israel's possessions were either confiscated or burned, in some strange way the writings of the prophets survived. Thousands of years have passed, but the messages delivered long ago may be found in our Bibles. This in itself is as great a miracle as any described in the Scriptures. There must be an explanation for this sensational preservation. God wrote and inspired the Bible, and it was essential for Him to preserve it. That is one reason why the Word of God will last forever.

Its matchless predictions

Many would-be prophets tried to predict the future, and sometimes their prophecies were fulfilled. There are people who claim to be able to read the stars, hands, and faces. At the beginning of each year, newspapers and magazines carry special articles that predict what may be expected. If a prophecy is fulfilled, special mention is made of the prophet, or prophetess, responsible for the prediction. If what is promised does not happen, the editors conveniently forget their mistake. This never happened with God's prophets. Everything predicted by the Lord's spokesmen came to pass, and even today it is possible to recognize predictions pertinent to our times being fulfilled around the world. This cannot be a coincidence. The prophets foretold the arrival of the Messiah, the place of His birth, the slaughter of children at His birth, His flight into Egypt, many details of His life, His death and resurrection, and subsequent return to earth. God's prophets never made a mistake. This claim can never be made concerning other forthtellers of the future. It is not a cause for amazement that the Bible has always outlived its critics.

Its marvelous power

The apostle Peter not only endorsed the claim that the Word of God would last forever, he said: "This is the word which by the gospel is preached unto you." His statement must be regarded as an astonishing utterance, for, since New Testament preachers agreed with the prophets, their messages were as inspired as those of the ancient preachers. This fact was endorsed by the miracles they performed. Paul wrote (Rom. 1:16), "For I am not ashamed of the gospel of Christ: for it is the power of God unto salvation to every one that believeth; to the Jew first, and also to the Greek." It has often been claimed that the greatest evidence *for* Christ is not the multiplicity of churches but the power that transforms men and women. One changed life is worth a ton of theology; one transformed home is to be more desired than a million sermons. Yet, in the providence of God, it is by the foolishness of preaching that He performs His amazing miracles. (See 1 Cor. 1:21.) When John the Baptist sent messengers to ask if Jesus was the Messiah and what proofs could be supplied to support His claim, the Lord replied, "Tell John what things ye have seen and heard, how that the blind see, the lame walk, and lepers are cleansed, the deaf hear, the dead are raised, to the poor the gospel is preached" (Luke 7:22). Then, and now, what Christ accomplishes in human hearts is of more worth than any opinion expressed about him. "Jesus Saves" is God's reply to a questioning world.

SOLOMON . . . who learned by observing

(PROVERBS 29:1)

One of the greatest attributes of wisdom is its ability to learn from many sources. Invariably, the man who knows everything knows little! Solomon was reputed to be the wisest of men, but even a casual glance at his writings enables the reader to know the king learned through observation. For example, many of his proverbs were studies in contrast; he compared extremes. It should be remembered that Solomon was close to his father and doubtless was acquainted with the events that made David's life memorable. He knew about King Saul and the details connected with the downfall of Israel's first king. He might have had Saul in mind when he wrote: "He that being often reproved hardeneth his neck, shall suddenly be destroyed, and that without remedy."

Constraining compassion . . . often reproved

Any person who repeatedly ignores warnings meant to prevent disaster asks for trouble. Drivers who ignore stop signs are injured or killed at intersections. People who ignore warnings within their bodies and refuse to seek medical advice are in a hurry to attend their own funeral! Children who in spite of parental instruction play with fire get burned. There are laws in life that are basic and must be observed. This fact applies in the spiritual realm. When Solomon remembered how God warned Saul, it became difficult to comprehend the actions of the monarch. Jealousy made him throw a javelin at a boy musician; increasing enmity destroyed the tranquility of his soul; and, when he refused to heed God's entreaties, he sank lower into the maelstrom of iniquity. That he was *often* reproved reflects the intensity of the love trying to save him. The same facts are expressed in the concern of God for every sinner. The mercy extended to guilty people appears to be endless; it only ceases when the final rescue operation has failed.

Continuing contempt . . . hardeneth his neck

Solomon was aware that Saul consistently refused to humble himself before God and consequently had deteriorated morally and spiritually. The same undeniable fact was evident in the life of Pharaoh, the king of Egypt. That ancient monarch had repeatedly hardened his heart until finally, so it is written, God hardened it. That meant the man was beyond the reconciling power of divine love; he was dead even before he died! Further effort was sure to fail, and therefore any additional attempt to evangelize his soul would increase his condemnation. Since there are to be degrees of punishment in eternity, the mercy of God ceases to strive with sinners to prevent increasing responsibility. No one knows when this takes place, and therefore it behooves people to heed the words of the Almighty: "Come *now*, and let us reason together, saith the LORD; though your sins be as scarlet, they shall be as white as snow . . ." (Isa. 1:18). God erects warning signs along the highways of life; the traveler who ignores them can only blame himself when he wrecks his soul.

Coming condemnation . . . "He . . . shall suddenly be destroyed."

King Solomon was aware of the tragedy that ruined Saul; the monarch's fall from divine favor was among the most pitiable events of all time. It was said of Saul, "The spirit of the LORD departed from [him]." (See 1 Sam. 16:14.) When the eternal night was approaching, the tormented man sought the aid of a witch and received further confirmation that his doom was imminent. There was something pathetic in the way Saul went to battle knowing he would never return. He was at a dead end; he could neither advance nor retreat; he was finished! We cannot help but wonder what might have happened if that unfortunate man had listened more attentively to the voice and entreaties of God.

His complete calamity . . . without remedy

If there be any sadness in eternity, it must be when God abandons a soul. There is no way by which to measure the love that permitted Christ to die for sinners; there is no way by which to assess the grief of God when, in spite of everything, He has to admit failure. "Without remedy" suggests the case is hopeless. When there is no remedy for a disease, there is no hope for the sufferer. When a final appeal for clemency is refused, a murderer has no star to brighten his sky; he must die. There is a finality in the statement "NO REMEDY"; it means nothing more can be done — not even by God; judgment becomes inevitable. Unfortunately, this was the case concerning sinners of Paul's generation. The apostle, writing to the church in Rome said of those practicing homosexuality: "For this cause God gave them up unto vile affections: for even their women did change the natural use into that which is against nature. And likewise also the men, leaving the natural use of the woman, burned in their lust one toward another; men with men working that which is unseemly, and *receiving in themselves that recompense of their error which was meet*. . . . God gave them over to a reprobate mind, to do those things which are not convenient" (Rom. 1:26-28). If Paul were here today, he would cite the dreaded disease AIDS as evidence to support his claim. The laws of God must be observed and honored. Solomon wrote: "Whoso breaketh an hedge, a serpent shall bite him" (Eccl. 10:8). Those who play with fire can expect to be burned. Solomon said so, and he was a wise man.

SOLOMON . . . who studied "little people"

(PROVERBS 30:25-28)

Great men never despise anything insignificant. They know little things can often be instructive. At one time in his life, David's best ally was a small pebble! Naaman's greatest friend was a small captive child brought from the land of Israel, and even a lad helped the Savior feed a large multitude. Some of God's greatest artistry has been displayed in minute forms; much of His wisdom was given to the unpretentious. Solomon considered insignificant creatures and recognized evidence of the creative power of an omniscient God.

The ants . . . their thoughtful preparation

"The ants are a people not strong, yet they prepare their meat in the summer." These tiny creatures are among the most defenseless beings in the world. A man's foot can kill hundreds of them in a moment; the long, probing tongue of the anteater can scoop up scores with one movement. The snow of winter can easily destroy a complete colony. Squirrels can hunt even when weather conditions are atrocious, but the infinitesimal ant must hide in the holes of the ground. Unable to survive in destructive frosts, it prepares in summer what is needed for winter. Procrastination would be suicidal. Solomon wrote, "Go to the ant, thou sluggard; consider her ways and be wise: Which having no guide, overseer or ruler, provideth her meat in the summer, and gathereth her food in the harvest" (Prov. 6:6-8). If the tiny ants could become evangelists, they would have ready-made sermons! They would advise people to prepare in life for eternity. They would probably ask, "If you neglect the present, How shalt thou do in the swellings of Jordan?" They are aware that laziness and unpreparedness are harbingers of doom.

The conies . . . their tremendous perception

"The conies are but a feeble folk, yet make they their houses in the rocks." These small animals possess God-given fur coats and are able to seek food at any time. Their danger comes from predators. They have no natural defense against the snapping teeth of larger animals; and, if they made their homes in bushes, trees, or on the ground, their lives would be brief. They know they are insufficient to overcome foes and therefore seek protection elsewhere. They scratch and claw their way into crevices in the rocks; they go as deep as possible so that huge boulders stand between them and danger. Solomon looked at the conies and saw wisdom. Enemies existed against which even he had no defense. Unfortunately, there came a time when the king was defeated by foes that arose within his own heart. Had he sheltered behind the Rock of Ages, he would not have been a prey to his passions. Blessed is the man or woman who recognizes inherent weakness and seeks refuge in time!

The locusts . . . their threatening problems

"The locusts have no king, yet they go forth all of them by bands." During Bible times, these creatures were the deadliest force known to man. Solomon could resist invading armies, but the arrival of locusts struck terror into an entire nation. Locusts had no military leader to direct action, no training sessions to prepare members for advances and conflict; there was never an organizing committee, but locusts never defected from the company. Their strength was unity; the secret of their invincibility was fellowship. Until science devised a way of combating these creatures with chemicals, they were the most formidable army ever to walk, crawl, or fly. They learned how to blitz an area; and, after they had gone, nothing remained but devastated fields and forests. Their methods were copied by armies which, when forced to retreat, "scorched the ground" so that advancing enemies would have nothing upon which to feed and no shelters in which to rest. Solomon recognized the unity of the locusts to be the secret of their success. He wondered why humans fought each other instead of helping. Peace is better than war; a helping hand is more effective than a blow. God made hands; unfortunately, men make fists!

The spiders . . . their tireless persistence

"The spider taketh hold with her hands, and is in kings' palaces." The spider is one of the most persistent creatures God ever created. It drops slowly from its elevated position on a tree or rafter; its tiny body suspended on a thin silken thread automatically produced as it descends. The creative creature ascends to another elevation slowly pulling its thread to make a bridge, and a web is formed around the solitary strand. It seems a tragedy when someone walks against the thread to break it. The spider then very methodically follows an identical procedure to restore what was destroyed. Armed guards protect places of importance, and intruders are either arrested or shot, but spiders gain entrance unmolested. Their motto seems to be, "If at first you don't succeed, try, try, and try again." Such insistence may be irritating, but it succeeds.

In Australia, I saw webs hanging from telephone wires and asked what they were. One old fellow replied, "Them be flyin' spiders, them be. They live in the swamps where the mosquitos live by the million. They eat them, but when the rains come, the area is flooded and those spiders would all be drowned, but they have brains! They make a webby-balloon and secure it by a single thread. At the first sign of danger, they sever the thread, and fly to higher ground. Them flyin' spiders have brains." Even Solomon would have coveted the wisdom of the tiny creatures that learned to fly!

SOLOMON . . . and his important question

(ECCLESIASTES 7:17)

"Why shouldest thou die before thy time?"

There exists in the minds of men a fatalism that can be deadly. It suggests there is a specific time when people must die. I do not believe it. A surgeon can delay the moment of death. A man's decision can delay it, and God can prevent it. Yet in every instance, responsibility rests upon the individual. He can refuse permission for a surgeon to operate; he may commit suicide and end his life prematurely, or he can hinder the working of God in his life. The Bible teaches it is possible for a person to die too early.

An awful possibility (Acts 5:1-10)

The Acts of the Apostles suggests the church resembled a benevolent society! *Jesus* was being preached, *jobs* were being lost, and *joy* was being experienced. As a result of these happenings (1) *Property* was being sold, (2) *People* were dedicated, and the (3) *Poor* were being helped. Then a man and his wife decided to deceive the apostles by selling their property and giving only a part of the sale price to the church fund. Their deception was very unwise; it cost them their lives. When Ananias, and later his wife, tried to deceive Simon Peter, the apostle said: "While it remained, was it not thine own? and after it was sold, was it not in thine own power? why hast thou conceived this thing in thine heart? thou hast not lied unto men, but unto God. And Ananias hearing these words fell down, and gave up the ghost: and great fear came on all them that heard these things" (Acts 5:4-5). About three hours later, the wife of Ananias suffered the same fate. Both died prematurely; they could have lived longer.

An awesome plea (2 Kings 2:11)

A nation was on its knees; the impossible had happened; revival was knocking at the door! Elijah, the mighty prophet of God, had won an amazing victory; after three years of drought, the life-giving rain was about to fall; the future was bright with promise and hope. What had taken place on Mount Carmel beggared description. The people would never forget the moment when the prophet of God said: "How long halt ye between two opinions? if the LORD be God, follow him: but if Baal, then follow him" (1 Kings 18:21). They had witnessed the failure of the false prophets and had seen the bullock placed on the altar by the man of God. His prayer had been electrifying: "Hear me, O LORD, hear me, that this people may know that thou art the LORD God, and that thou hast turned their heart back again.... Then the fire of the LORD fell'' (1 Kings 18:37-38). It all seemed like a dream; God had rescued His people. ''And Ahab told Jezebel all that Elijah had done.... Then Jezebel sent a message unto Elijah, saying, So let the gods do to me, and more also, if I make not thy life as the life of one of them by tomorrow about this time. And when [Elijah] saw that, he arose, and went for his life'' (1 Kings 19:1-3). Poor man! At that moment he committed suicide; his ministry abruptly terminated. He might have led a nation into the fullness of the blessing of God, but had he tried, the people would have laughed at him. God removed Elijah when he was needed very much on earth. He lost the greatest opportunity of his life!

An assured promise (2 Kings 20:1-6)

The king's palace was very silent; servants moved quietly; they spoke in whispers. Hezekiah was dying. They watched as the prophet Isaiah walked somberly toward the royal bedroom; they were scared, for the man of God was not smiling. His face gave warning of doom. They were correct, for Isaiah went to the sick monarch to say: ''Set thine house in order; for thou shalt die, and not live.'' ''Then [the king] turned his face to the wall, and prayed unto the LORD, saying, I beseech thee, O LORD, remember now how I have walked before thee in truth and with a perfect heart, and have done that which is good in thy sight. And Hezekiah wept sore.'' Was this the fateful moment when his time to die had arrived? Yes and no! ''And it came to pass, afore Isaiah was gone out into the middle court, that the word of the LORD came to him, saying, Turn again, and tell Hezekiah . . . Thus saith the LORD . . . I will add unto thy days fifteen years; and I will deliver thee.'' No man is indispensable to God, but it is wise to live so that He will think we are! It should be remembered that, when Daniel spoke to king Belshazzar, he said, ''And *the God in whose hand thy breath is*, and whose are all thy ways, hast thou not glorified'' (Dan. 5:23).

Long life may be dependent upon spirituality. David knew this, for in Psalm 91, speaking of the man who prayed faithfully to God, he quoted a divine promise, ''With long life will I satisfy him, and show him my salvation'' (v. 16). If you wish to live long . . . live right!

ISAIAH . . . and his magnificent word pictures

(ISAIAH 32:2)

Isaiah was one of the major prophets, and his word pictures were unsurpassed. Evidently he was acquainted with the wilderness areas of his country and realized desert storms offered no comfort. When particles of sand were driven by gale force winds into the faces of travelers, problems multiplied. The wilderness offered no comfort, and travelers who failed to reach an oasis prior to a storm were in jeopardy. When Isaiah looked ahead to the arrival of the Messiah, he saw the Coming One silhouetted against the somber background of a sandstorm, and his description of that event made exciting reading.

A sheltered place

"And a man shall be as an hiding place from the wind and a covert from the tempest." When a traveler was overtaken by a desert storm, he could make his camel lie down with its back to the wind, and crouching at the side of the beast, try to hide from flying sand. This was a very poor shelter, but it was better than nothing. The fortunate people who were at an oasis sought refuge behind primitive fences or barricades, or even in a strengthened tent, but to be besieged in a desert was tragic. Possibly the prophet knew this experience and delivered his text with increased emphasis. Later in 42:13, Isaiah said, "The LORD shall go forth as a mighty man." He saw the Lord of heaven coming to live upon the earth, and his vision of the Messiah was marvelous. Did he understand what Christ meant to imply when the Lord said, "Come unto me, all ye that labour and are heavy laden, and I will give you rest. Take my yoke upon you, and learn of me; for I am meek and lowly in heart: and ye shall find rest unto your souls?" (Matt. 11:28-29). This was the immortal picture of a young, rebellious ox being helped by an older animal. When ploughing was difficult and the young ox was incapable of doing its job, the older beast gently assumed the responsibility of pulling the plough so that the younger one could rest. Isaiah foresaw the coming of God's Man, who would be a hiding place in a torturous desert. In Him, people would find shelter from the threatening storms of life.

A sustaining place

"A man shall be . . . as rivers of water in a dry place." There is little if any water in a desert. Nomadic tribesmen might know of secret places where supplies can be found, but outside of an oasis water is almost non-existent. Isaiah described the world as a desert where living water was unobtainable. Then he described how God's Man would come to earth and be "as rivers of water in a dry place."

It is interesting that he described the supplies as "rivers." There would be enough for every thirsty traveler. Perhaps the Lord had this prediction in His mind when on "The last day, that great day of the feast, [He] stood and cried, saying, If any man thirst, let him come unto me, and drink" (John 7:37). Speaking with the woman at Sychar's well, Jesus said, "Whosoever drinketh of this water shall thirst again: But whoso drinketh of the water that I shall give him shall never thirst; but the water that I shall give him shall be in him a well of water springing up into everlasting life" (John 4:13-14). Men dying of thirst in a desert would never refuse to drink when water became available. It is incomprehensible that sinners in urgent need of living water should be hesitant about accepting supplies which only Christ offers. To accept the Savior is to live; to refuse His gift is to die. Jesus said, "And let him that is athirst come. And whosoever will, let him take the water of life freely" (Rev. 22:17).

A safe place

"And a man shall be . . . as the shadow of a great rock in a weary land." There are some rocky promontories in a desert, but unfortunately these are often buried by shifting sand. What could be a hiding place often becomes unavailable. It is therefore significant that Isaiah described the Messiah to be *a great rock.* It is something permanent, something that changing circumstances could never obliterate. It would always be there, a shelter in a storm, a landmark to guide travelers through the wilderness. It would remain an enduring, indispensable gift of God. The Rock of Ages would withstand any storm and last eternally. All people would be safe in its shadow; it would stand tall; all who looked would easily see it! "And the eyes of them that see shall not be dim, and the ears of them that hear shall hearken" (Isa. 32:3).

When Augustus Toplady was overtaken by a storm in Somersetshire, England, he climbed into a crevice in the nearby rocks and there, sheltered from the wind and rain, remembered the Lord was a hiding place. He wrote,

Rock of Ages, cleft for me,
Let me hide myself in Thee.

When Charles Wesley composed the hymn, "Jesus, Lover of My Soul," he was inspired by a small bird which, chased by a predator, flew through an open window to take refuge in the preacher's unbuttoned jacket. Wesley was so impressed that he wrote,

Jesus, Lover of my soul,
Let me to Thy bosom fly,
While the nearer waters roll,
While the tempest still is high!

Hide me, O my Savior, hide
Till the storm of life is past,
Safe into the haven guide,
O receive my soul at last!

Blessed indeed is the soul that hides in the Rock of Ages.

JEREMIAH . . . who looked ahead and asked a question (JEREMIAH 12:5)

A person's attitude toward time often reveals the state of his soul. Some men enjoy living in the past, for neither the present nor the future has any interest for them. Others live only for the present; they ignore the past and, utterly indifferent to what the future might bring, live only for "the now." To them, the past has gone and the future may never come; therefore they enjoy what is and ignore all else. A third class lives mostly for the future and devotes time to preparing for tomorrow! They do their best to learn from the mistakes of yesterday; they endeavor to enjoy today but, wishing to avoid embarrassment of any kind, carefully prepare for any forthcoming eventuality. The question might be asked, "Which is the wisest of the three?" Jeremiah lived among people who almost exclusively belonged to the second type. They lived only for the present, and the prophet, recognizing the inherent weakness of their philosophy, asked an important question, "How wilt thou do in the swelling of Jordan?"

It was a reasonable question . . . death was sure!

The rising and overflowing of the Jordan River was an event of considerable importance in Israel. Within a land where water was never plentiful, every effort had to be made to conserve supplies whenever they became available. "The former and the latter rains" represented periods in the year when the precious rain fell upon a very dry land. The river Jordan, which was always the lifeline for Israel, steadily rose until the water overflowed its banks to flood adjacent pasture lands. The Hebrew farmers, anticipating the event, made preparations for the irrigation of their lands. Some of the men even placed seed upon the spreading water so that the planting could be done in an economical manner. Using this as an illustration of death sweeping over the nation and stressing the fact that the event was impossible to prevent, Jeremiah asked what the people were doing to prepare for the future. He said, "If thou hast run with the footmen, and they have wearied thee, then how canst thou contend with horses? and if in the land of peace, wherein thou trustedst, they wearied thee, then how wilt thou do in the swelling of Jordan?" He seemed to be saying, "You are not doing too well when everything is in your favor; so what will happen when everything goes wrong?"

It was a thoughtful question . . . preparation was necessary!

The prophet drew attention to incidents that every listener could comprehend. He asked: "If you are unhappy in times of prosperity, what will you do when adversity overwhelms you? If money cannot buy peace, what will you do when you have no money? If you make no preparation in life, what will happen when death takes you away?" His pungent remarks should have brought Israel to her senses, but alas, the people were so indifferent to the claims of God that, in spite of everything, they were forced into captivity. One of the prophets had said, "If God be for us, who can be against us?" but when God withdrew His aid from the sinful nation, the outlook became intensely bleak. The old adage was proved to be true — "One never misses the water until the well runs dry!" Against these sordid facts, the question might be asked, "What preparation can be made to prepare for eternity?" Jesus supplied the answer. He said, "I am the resurrection, and the life: he that believeth in me, though he were dead, yet shall he live. And whosoever liveth and believeth in me, shall never die" (John 11:25-26).

It was an important question . . . delay was dangerous!

Jeremiah lived in an age when there was no meteorological service giving daily forecasts of expected weather conditions. Farmers had to make their own predictions. That explains why the Lord said to the Pharisees: "When it is evening, ye say, It will be fair weather: for the sky is red. And in the morning, It will be foul weather today: for the sky is red and lowering. O ye hypocrites, ye can discern the face of the sky; but can ye not discern the signs of the times?" (Matt. 16:2-3). At certain periods during the year, it was possible for the Jordan to overflow without warning, and therefore farmers had to be prepared for unexpected eventualities. Indifference or delay could result in bankruptcy. Jeremiah was aware that this could happen in more senses than one. The final journey from time into eternity would be taken by each listener; and, unless preparation was made, their stupidity would become evident to everybody. The intensity of the prophet's conviction warned sinners of their precarious position. To be caught unprepared for the greatest crisis in life would be the forerunner of eternal disaster.

EZEKIEL . . . the prophet who went on strike

(EZEKIEL 3:15)

We live in an age when strikes are commonplace. All branches of industry can be paralyzed when workers become dissatisfied with working conditions. It is thought-provoking that clergymen never emulate the modern trend. Maybe they are too satisfied or too scared to strike lest they lose their employment permanently! It is interesting to discover that, although the Bible mentions false and true prophets and some that ran away from responsibilities, only one preacher ever decided to strike against God.

The false profession

Ezekiel was one of the captives in Babylon; he was highly esteemed by the elders who constantly consulted with him on matters of religious importance. It would appear from his statements that he was proud of his people, for their profession of faith in Jehovah was constant and strong. Their idols had been destroyed, their commitment to God and Jerusalem had been maintained, and it was only a matter of time before God would restore them to their own land. Psalm 137:1-5 supplies the following wonderful picture of the attitude of the captives: "By the rivers of Babylon, there we sat down, yea, we wept, when we remembered Zion. We hanged our harps upon the willows in the midst thereof. For there they that carried us away captive required of us a song; and they that wasted us required of us mirth, saying, Sing us one of the songs of Zion. How shall we sing the LORD'S song in a strange land? If I forget thee, O Jerusalem, let my right hand forget her cunning." Yes, Ezekiel must have been very proud of his fellow captives; they were the chosen people of Jehovah; it was a privilege to minister to them. The prophet apparently failed to recognize that somewhere, something was wrong!

The furious prophet

When Ezekiel received a new commission from God, he could not believe his ears! "And he said unto me, Son of man, go, and get thee unto the house of Israel, and speak with my words unto them . . . But the house of Israel will not hearken unto thee; for they will not hearken unto me; for all the house of Israel is stiff of forehead and hard of heart" (marginal reading; Ezek. 3:4,7). Ezekiel probably considered this to be outrageous! His flock had learned their lesson. They needed encouragement, not condemnation. The more the prophet considered the situation, the more he believed God was unfair, and suddenly Ezekiel began to sulk. He could not chastise people who were doing their utmost to be holy in a heathen land.

Later he wrote, "I went in bitterness, in the heat of my spirit. . . . and I sat where they sat, and remained there astonished [silent] among them seven days" (Ezek. 3:14-15).

The filthy pictures

It will always be a cause for thanksgiving that God's patience lasts longer than the indiscretions of His people. Ezekiel temporarily quit his job, but the Lord was very understanding. "The hand of the LORD was strong upon me" (3:14). God gave to the prophet a vision in which he was taken to the temple and instructed to dig a hole in the outside wall. When he reached a door, he was told to enter and behold the secret abomination of the religious leaders. "So I went in and saw; and behold every form of creeping things, and abominable beasts, and all the idols of the house of Israel, portrayed upon the wall round about. . . . Then said he unto me, Son of man, hast thou seen what the ancients of the house of Israel do in the dark, every man in the chambers of his imagery? for they say, The LORD seeth us not . . . " (Ezek. 8:7-12). The prophet's strike came to an abrupt end. He realized the secret sins of the priests were destroying the nation.

The frightening prediction

When the prophet resumed his ministry, his warnings were unmistakable; his spirit had been stirred when he recognized the hypocrisy of those who sinned in the dark. He stressed the important truth that, unless they repented, the future would be exceedingly bleak. The Bible asserts that believers are the temple of the Holy Spirit, and there exists the possibility that if Ezekiel lived today he might want to dig a hole in our walls. Do we permit prohibited pictures to hang upon the inner walls of the sanctuary or allow idols to stand in the holy place? It is impossible to hide anything from God, and prudence suggests the advisability of obeying His command. "If my people, which are called by my name, shall humble themselves, and pray, and seek my face, and turn from their wicked ways; then will I hear from heaven, and will forgive their sin, and will heal their land" (2 Chron. 7:14). What we really are speaks far more eloquently than anything we say. True revival begins in the secret places of the human temple.

THE MEN AND THE MASTER . . . who stood in the gap for God (Ezekiel 22:30)

"And I sought for a man among them, that should make up the hedge, and stand in the gap before me for the land, that I should not destroy it: but I found none." All the cities of Palestine, during Bible times, were surrounded by walls. Sheepfolds and gardens were also protected either by walls or hedges. When Nehemiah restored Jerusalem, each family was assigned a certain part of the construction. There were enemies outside who constantly sought to find a gap in the defenses of the city so that the restoration would be hindered. The prophet's utterance was easily understood; it was a word picture of an everyday occurrence.

A pattern shattered (Ezek. 22:30)

The history of the human race suggests that God was always searching for someone able to "stand in the gap." Adam was created to rescue a planet that had been ruined, possibly by the fall of Lucifer. The earth was recreated and Adam instructed to replenish it. Noah was required to stand in the gap for a sinful world; he built the ark, and sailed through the flood waters. Abraham was asked to do likewise for a decadent people, and later Moses stood in the gap for a wayward nation. After many years, God found a boy named Samuel, and that lad became a savior for Israel. David also was appointed to stand in a military gap for the nation; he saved them from extinction. God was always able to find a suitable instrument to meet the need of a particular generation; but, alas, during the life of Ezekiel, God failed in His search. There was not a man able to stand in the gap and save the nation from the advancing Babylonians. "And I sought for a man among them . . . but I found none." The text seems to imply that God had reached an impasse; He had run out of human material! The Babylonian danger was insignificant when compared with the threat occasioned by a world's iniquity. Who could stand in the gap between God's holiness and man's sin? Obviously, no man could do this, for all had sinned.

A problem solved (Phil. 2:5-8)

Angels were unworthy of, and incapable of, the task of saving sinners from destruction. The only course of action remaining for God was to supply *His own Man.* The Holy Spirit moved within the life of Mary, and she became the instrument by which the Son of God came to earth. Once again God was commencing with a child. When Jesus became an adult, it became increasingly noticable that He was different from all other men. He was "one of a kind" and was standing in the gap for God. Later, He was called a *stone* — the chief cornerstone, which united walls and supported a structure.

He was called a *shepherd* — the Shepherd who sought lost sheep. Finally He was called a *Savior,* who at the cost of His life, stood in the gap for God and brought salvation to undeserving sinners. Then, and only then, could it be said that God had filled the gap between the requirements of divine law and the appalling guilt of sinners.

A position secured (Heb. 10:12)

"But this man, after he had offered one sacrifice for sins for ever, sat down on the right hand of God." What a Man! The letter to the Hebrews refers to *This Man* and contrasts Him with His predecessors. Jesus was different in *His consecration.* All the men previously found by God to stand in a gap failed because of their sinfulness. Abraham became a liar. Moses became a victim of temper and lost the privilege of entering the Promised Land. David became a victim of his own passion and murdered a faithful husband. Elijah became a coward and ruined his ministry. Yet Jesus had been tempted in all points as we are and had triumphed gloriously.

Jesus was different in *His continuity.* There had been many wonderful priests who succeeded Aaron, but they had died. Not one had been able to complete what he began. "And they truly were many priests, because they were not suffered to continue by reason of death. But this man [Jesus], because he continueth ever, hath an unchangeable priesthood. Wherefore he is able also to save them to the uttermost that come unto God by him, seeing he ever liveth to make intercession for them" (Heb. 7:23-25).

Finally this glorious Savior, who stands in our stead before God, was different in *His completeness.* The Old Testament priests were themselves sinners, and it was necessary to make atonement for their sins before they attempted to intercede for others. That can never happen again, for our High Priest is now seated at the right hand of the Majesty on high and will never be replaced. "He ever liveth to make intercession for [us]." Ancient men stood in the gap for a limited period of time; the Savior eternally stands in the gap for those who trust Him. This glorious message suggests three vital truths. It *provides peace, promises protection,* and *promotes praise.* That probably explains why the writer to the Hebrews called it "So great salvation." (See Heb. 2:3.)

HOSEA . . . who bought his wife at an auction

(HOSEA 3:1-2)

To understand the life and ministry of Hosea, it is necessary to be acquainted with the times in which he lived. Israel was enjoying great prosperity, there was only one official place of worship in the land, and the appearance of a prophet was a cause for national interest. Often the people remained indifferent to what he preached, but they were interested in his actions.

Love hoping

Hosea fell in love with a fashionable young woman of the social set in Israel and was married in Samaria. Within a year, his son was born and named Jezreel in memory of one of Israel's greatest battlefields. The proud father probably hoped his boy would become a famous general in the army. The wife, whose name was Gomer, had probably been infatuated with her famous sweetheart, and for a time at least all went well within their home.

Love hurting

Eventually, former associates returned to enslave Gomer's soul, and she became unfaithful. She gave birth to two other children, but Hosea was not their father. The names given to the children were very suggestive. *Lo-ruhamah* meant "Not loved"; *Lo-ammi* meant "Not my kin." When Gomer finally deserted her family to return to her lovers, Hosea became father and mother to three small children. His love was indeed hurting, but there is no record that he ever tried to divorce his disgusting partner.

Love helping

After years had passed, Hosea received tragic news. Gomer had been abandoned by her friends and, unable to pay her debts, was about to be sold into slavery. He hurried to the slave market and must have been shocked by the changed appearance of his wife. The attractive young lady of earlier years had become a worn, faded, undesired woman who had aged prematurely. Possibly after some bartering, the prophet was able to buy back his wife. He had very little money; but, if the auctioneer would be cooperative, Hosea would add to the purchase price one-and-a-half homers of barley. When this was agreed, he gave his fifteen pieces of silver and later added the barley, and the transaction was completed. When Hosea took the woman back into his heart and home, it was certainly one of the strangest homecomings ever to take place.

Love healing

It was very significant when the names of the children were changed to Ruhamah and Ammi. They were now "Loved" and "My kin." True love within the heart of that saintly man was healing the wounds that had been inflicted upon his soul. The fact that Hosea welcomed Gomer back was indicative that, in spite of her sin, he still loved her.

Love heralding

Hosea wondered why all these things had happened to him. In time, God revealed the reasons for all the misfortunes. What Gomer had been to Hosea, Israel had been, and still was, to God. As the prophet considered the implications of this revelation, he discovered that God had a heart! When he resumed preaching, new notes could be heard in his voice and message. What he preached afterward may be condensed into three vital but simple headings.

God's problem

The question: "How shall I give thee up, Ephraim? how shall I deliver thee, Israel?" (11:8) indicated that as Hosea had suffered because of the evil conduct of his wife, so God had suffered because of the waywardness of His people. Hosea was able to understand and appreciate the yearnings in the heart of God, because he had experienced similar sorrow.

God's pity

"O Israel, thou hast destroyed thyself; but in me is thine help" (v. 13:9). These words could have been spoken by Hosea when he rushed to speak with his wife, as she stood helplessly at the auctioneer's table. Pity, and not anger, filled his heart. Then, as Hosea reminisced, he saw not Gomer, but the entire nation. They also had run away from God and had committed adultery with false lovers. Yet, in spite of their indiscretions, God continued to love His backslidden people. When Hosea began to preach his new message, the denunciations were not as harsh; love was mellowing both the preacher and the message.

God's promise

Hosea's soul must have been thrilled when the Lord whispered, "I will heal their backsliding, I will love them freely; for mine anger is turned away from him" (14:4). It should be remembered that all these wonderful verses are found at the end of Hosea's book. They were produced out of his own deep, personal sorrow. Then, and only then, did the prophet understand the sermon that had been produced in his life. Hosea's message was never the same again. He had discovered that God could sincerely love sinners.

JOEL . . . Mr. Nobody from nowhere

Read Joel 1:4-12. Modern people might be inclined to call this prophet Mr. John Doe. He was unknown until certain events thrust him upon the central stage of Israel's life. It may be assumed from his writings that he lived near the temple area; some writers think he was a temple prophet. He certainly lived in Jerusalem and ministered prior to the Babylonian captivity. There are three chapters in his book, and each has its own distinctive message.

A terrible plight

At the time of his ministry, Israel was being ruined by a terrible plague of locusts (2:1-11). They ran along streets and climbed walls; and, when they moved through the air, even the sun appeared to be eclipsed. Yet in adjacent countries the scourge was not present, and even the most outrageous sinners prospered. To many of the pious inhabitants of Israel, this appeared to be unfair. The situation described by Joel was exceedingly frightening, and all the ladies in Israel must have been very scared. The locusts were in their houses, among their clothing, and even contaminated their food. The farmers were desperate, for within hours harvests were being destroyed, and the economic future of the nation was in jeopardy. Then suddenly Joel made his appearance. Little is known about him except that the Holy Spirit anointed the man and within a very short time an unknown preacher became a person of national prominence.

A tremendous plea

Joel said: "Blow ye the trumpet in Zion, and sound an alarm in my holy mountain: let all the inhabitants of the land tremble: for the day of the LORD cometh, for it is nigh at hand" (2:1). Whether or not the rulers of the city did as the prophet suggested, we do not know, but later he repeated his demand (2:15). "Blow the trumpet in Zion, sanctify a fast, call a solemn assembly. Gather the people, sanctify the congregation, assemble the elders, gather the children, and those that suck the breasts . . . . Let the priests, the ministers of the LORD, weep between the porch and the altar, and let them say, Spare thy people, O LORD . . . . Then will the LORD be jealous for his land, and pity his people" (2:15-18). The rulers saw only the problems threatening the country; Joel saw God waiting to help those who called upon His name.

This plea from the lips of Joel is probably among the greatest recorded in the Scriptures. The people were in tremendous danger, but there was nothing too hard for the Lord. If only the people would turn to God, anything would become possible. Probably Joel had often read the prayer offered by Solomon at the dedication of the temple and shared the assurance that filled the king's heart. God could help the people if they turned to Him in prayer. It is interesting to note that everyone was included in Joel's suggestion. Even the youngest babies were to be brought before God. It was true that such infants would be unaware of the importance of the occasion, but their presence would be an indication of the obedience of their parents.

A thrilling promise

It was at some point during this man's ministry that he suddenly began to widen the scope of his message. He became aware of a large world, and a new concept filled his soul. He spoke of the day when the Lord would pour out His Spirit upon mankind and, mentioning the strange signs to appear in the heavens, described how multitudes would be in the valley of decision. The Lord would "roar out of Zion!" It is probable that Joel did not understand the tremendous importance of all he uttered, but his prediction was destined to become famous. Long afterward, when the Holy Spirit came to revolutionize the disciples and make possible the evangelizing of the nations, Peter, explaining the phenomenon, said, "But this is that which was spoken by the prophet Joel" (Acts 2:16).

"And it shall come to pass in that day, that the mountains shall drop down new wine, and the hills shall flow with milk, and all the rivers of Judah shall flow with waters" (3:18). "So shall ye know that I am the LORD your God dwelling in Zion, my holy mountain: then shall Jerusalem be holy, and there shall no strangers pass through her any more" (3:17). Joel saw the light shining at the end of a long tunnel. He was an obscure, but wonderful, servant of God.

AMOS . . . the preacher from the south

After the death of King Solomon, the nation of Israel was divided into two sections. The northern kingdom had its capital at Bethel where the king's chapel became the center of the country. The southern kingdom was centered in Jerusalem, and for many years these two areas were totally opposed. Amos belonged to the southern kingdom. He lived in the village of Tekoa, twelve miles from Jerusalem and eighteen miles from the Dead Sea, where the land was barren. He earned his living by tending cattle and sheep, but as a sideline increased his income by dressing sycamore trees. He was just an ordinary farm worker, and no one would have dreamed he would become a prophet. When later he was required to speak before the king, he said, "I was no prophet, neither was I a prophet's son; but I was an herdman, and a gatherer of sycamore fruit: And the LORD took me as I followed the flock, and the LORD said unto me, Go, prophesy unto my people Israel" (Amos 7:14-15).

The amazing preacher . . . God's complaint

It was the time of the annual festival at Bethel. The city and the king's chapel were crowded with important people. The rich, the famous, and the politicians were gathered to celebrate the special event. Doubtless the singing was beautiful, the meetings attractive, and those who had arranged the celebrations were thrilled. Then one day a strange, bewildering man walked into the assembly. His garments smelled of fields and animals; it was easy to recognize he was a stranger to perfume! When he began to preach, everybody recognized him to be a prophet. He denounced the sins of the adjacent countries; and, if it were customary in those days to express religious emotion, the place soon echoed with "Amens." "Glory be to God, this man can surely preach!" The entire congregation was fascinated and thrilled until Amos, the man from the south, began to denounce the sins of the northern kingdom. The smiles of appreciation were quickly replaced by scowls. "This fool is a meddler! It was fine when he denounced others, but by whose authority does he criticize us?"

The annoyed priest . . . God's challenge

"Then Amaziah the priest of Bethel sent to Jeroboam king of Israel, saying, Amos hath conspired against thee in the midst of the house of Israel: the land is not able to bear all his words. For thus Amos saith, Jeroboam shall die by the sword, and Israel shall surely be led away captive out of their own land" (7:10-11). It seems easy to understand the priest's predicament. This bewildering preacher from across the border had become a nuisance; his message was not good for the morale of the country. Apparently the priest gave no attention to God's message. Amos had said: "Seek not Bethel, nor . . . Gilgal, and pass not to Beer-sheba. . . . Seek the LORD, and ye shall live" (5:5-6). When God warned of threatening disaster, He also revealed a way of escape. Alas, the pride of the priest had been hurt; his name had been mentioned by the interfering prophet. Then "Amaziah said unto Amos, O thou seer, go, flee thee away into the land of Judah, and there eat bread, and prophesy there: But prophesy not again any more at Bethel: for it is the king's chapel, and it is the king's court" (7:12-13). He seemed to say, "In this house of dignity we do not appreciate noisy preachers. Your type of message is not acceptable in this revered sanctuary." Amos was a man before our time. If he came back today he would recognize the scenery!

The astonishing promises . . . God's commitments

The record of the preaching of Amos is very thought-provoking. Each chapter of his book contains a distinctive message, but probably the last is the greatest of all. From verse 9 to the end of the chapter, there are several "I wills." It became obvious that the hand of God rested heavily upon the herdman from Tekoa, for his vision encompassed eternity. It is interesting to count the predictions of God and to recognize His promises. "Behold, the days come, saith the LORD, that the plowman shall overtake the reaper, and the treader of grapes him that soweth seed; and the mountains shall drop sweet wine, and all the hills shall melt" (9:13). True repentance was, and still is, the key that unlocks heaven's treasure house. Amos was only a poor farmer, but he supplied evidence that God can choose foolish things to confound the wise and weak things to confound the mighty! (See 1 Cor. 1:27.)

OBADIAH . . . who didn't like his cousins

(OBADIAH 3-4)

The Book of Obadiah may appear to be insignificant when compared with other prophetical writings; its solitary chapter may seem devoid of interest. Nevertheless, the preaching of this man against the fortress of Selah (or Edom) becomes alive with meaning when the background of his ministry is understood. The mysterious city of Petra is today the greatest tourist attraction in Jordan. Plans are being made to reconstruct parts of this fortress so that it will become the most fascinating place on earth. Its history dates back to the time of Solomon, and to walk down the narrow slit in the earth, to find and explore the hidden valley, is an unforgettable experience. The Edomites who were the original inhabitants of Petra were descendants of Esau and were therefore distant cousins of the Jewish people. They named their capital city "Selah," which meant *the rock.* It was a fortress created by God when a mighty earthquake split the earth. A very narrow canyon, one mile long and four hundred feet deep, was its only entrance. The pass was so narrow at the base that one man could hold it against an army. A careful reading of the indictment made by Obadiah reveals the reasons for his predicted judgment on the inhabitants of this ancient citadel.

God's timely prophet

Nothing is known about Obadiah's home, early life, or his upbringing. His name was among the most common in Old Testament times, but that God could take and use a man of such little consequence indicates He can take ordinary people and confound the mighty! When Obadiah came on the prophetical scene, Selah, or Petra as it is now called, was considered to be impregnable. Innumerable caves had been cut in the cliffs, and its population exceeded three thousand people. Later, when the fortress was captured by the Nabateans, they also carved in the red cliffs, and the "Treasury" which stands at the end of the valley is one of the most illustrious monuments of all time. Obadiah doubtless had been in this citadel and was well acquainted with its details.

God's troubled people

When heathens attacked the Jews and devastated the city of Jerusalem, the Edomites gloated over the fall of the Hebrews and participated in their defeat. When the young men of Israel tried to escape down the wadies in the desert, the inhabitants of Selah cut the escape routes and made some of the young Jews slaves. Surplus captives were sold to the conquering invaders when the strange cousins of Judah exploited their misfortune. Obadiah was incensed with all these treacherous people, and his voice echoed among the cliffs as he denounced the slave traders.

God's tremendous power

Some of the statements of the little-known prophet were very potent. "Thou shouldest not have entered into the gate of my people in the day of their calamity; yea, thou shouldest not have looked on their affliction . . . nor have laid hands on their substance . . . Neither shouldest thou have stood in the crossway, to cut off those of his that did escape; neither shouldest thou have delivered up those of his that did remain in the day of distress" (vv. 13-14). The Edomites were proud, self-reliant, and confident. They were safe; their fortress could not fall. They were mistaken. Selah was ultimately captured. The words of Obadiah were very expressive. "The pride of thine heart hath deceived thee, thou that dwellest in the clefts of the rock, whose habitation is high; that saith in his heart, Who shall bring me down to the ground? Though thou exalt thyself as an eagle, and though thou set thy nest among the stars, thence will I bring thee down, saith the LORD" (vv. 3-4).

God's thrilling promises

Having delivered his denunciation of the contemptible cousins of Israel, Obadiah began to speak of the ultimate glory of the defeated Jews. He mentioned several thrilling details of what would happen and described how God would bring "saviors" to help His despondent people. His final statement, "and the kingdom shall be the LORD'S," harmonized with the predictions of all other prophets that, in the end of time, "the King would come to Zion." This assured everybody that not even the wickedness of men could thwart the purposes of the Almighty. Obadiah was a brave man; it remains a mystery how he escaped the wrath of his enemies. Were they afraid to kill a prophet of God? Were God's protective arms around His faithful servant? We may not know the answers to these questions, but one thing seems obvious. God is capable of sheltering all who faithfully serve Him.

JONAH . . . who couldn't run fast enough

(JONAH 1)

The story of Jonah has engaged the attention of the church in all ages. Theologians argued about its interpretation, scoffers sneered at its message, but everybody, for one reason or another, found it interesting. There are three schools of interpretation. (1) Those who *Deny and Destroy* it. They state it is unacceptable because it is not based on historical fact. They say it is only a legend, an allegory suggesting truth. (2) There are others who *Doubt and Distort* it. They affirm it is a parable, a story with an application. Jonah was swallowed by the fish god of Babylon, and his experiences illustrate the seventy years of captivity known by Israel. (3) There are others who *Defend and Declare* it to be the Word of God. Jesus was among that number, for He said that, as Jonah was three days and nights in the belly of the fish, so would He be in the heart of the earth. That Jonah was a real man with a real ministry is seen from 2 Kings 14:25.

The stubborn soul

Jonah the prophet was commissioned by God to go to Nineveh to denounce the sins of the people who lived there. "But Jonah rose up to flee unto Tarshish from the presence of the LORD, and went down to Joppa; and he found a ship going to Tarshish; so he paid the fare thereof, and went down into it, to go with them unto Tarshish from the presence of the LORD." The question has often been asked, Why did Jonah do this? Three replies have been forthcoming. (1) He was a bigoted Jew refusing to have any association with a Gentile city. (2) He was a coward and feared the brutality of the Ninevites. The British Museum in London, England, has many exhibits that depict the ferocity of the Ninevites of Jonah's generation. Bronze and marble statues show them plunging spears into defenseless victims; they were people without mercy. (3) Other teachers affirm that Jonah was a brave man who was willing, for Israel's sake, to sacrifice his soul. Jonah, so it is said, knew the Ninevites were planning to invade Israel and that their ultimate victory was assured. He therefore refused to urge repentance, hoping God would destroy Nineveh before its citizens destroyed Israel.

The stormy sea

The law stated that, if a watchman was aware of approaching danger and neglected to warn a threatened city and if the city fell, the blood of its slain citizens would be required at the hands of the negligent watchman. Jonah, by refusing to warn Nineveh, became subject to that law. If Nineveh perished, its blood would be upon the soul of the preacher who was aware of the danger but gave no warning. However meritorious his motive might have been, the actions of the disobedient prophet threatened to destroy his soul. Jonah was aware of this fact but persisted in running from his duty. Alas, he could not outrun God. Having purchased a passage on the ship bound for Tarshish in Spain, the runaway preacher retired to the lower deck to sleep. He did not realize God was already on the ship. The Lord issued a silent command and the waves became tempestuous. The ship was thrown around as if it had been a cork, and yet Jonah never awakened. He was content; even God could not catch him now! Poor man! He was very tired, but he was also sick — in his soul.

The startled seamen

When the captain of the ship gently shook the sleeping prophet to ask, "What meanest thou, O sleeper?" and when the crew discovered by casting lots that Jonah was the cause of their peril, they began pestering him with questions. Fears and superstition ruined their peace of mind; they did not wish to die prematurely. When Jonah asked to be thrown overboard, he probably did so with sullen delight. "Yes, drown me; the sooner I die, the more quickly I shall be beyond the reach of God." Probably his conscience was already reminding him of the inadvisability of trying to outrun the Lord. David discovered the same truth. He wrote: "Whither shall I go from thy spirit? . . . If I take the wings of the morning, and dwell in the uttermost parts of the sea; Even there shall thy hand lead me, and thy right hand shall hold me" (Ps. 139:7-10).

The subdued speaker

"So they took up Jonah, and cast him forth into the sea: and the sea ceased from her raging. Then the men feared the LORD exceedingly, and offered a sacrifice . . . Now the LORD had prepared a great fish to swallow up Jonah. And Jonah was in the belly of the fish three days and three nights" (1:15-17). Poor man! He had the surprise of his life. The story is eloquent in its details. God commanded the waves and they obeyed Him; God used Jonah as a preacher to the seamen, and "they offered a sacrifice and made vows." Yet, at the same time, the Lord was dealing with His rebellious preacher and making him what he should have been from the beginning. It is never safe nor wise to flee from responsibility; a sense of duty is inextricably woven into our conscience. Poor Jonah, he had a lot to learn — and so do we.

JONAH . . . who prayed in a fish

(JONAH 2)

The word "but" occurs eight times in this book, and each time represents a "turn in the road." It is interesting to find and study each one. For example, there is the "but" of *Disobedience* in 1:3, of *Decision* in 1:4, of *Displeasure* in 1:5. These three in turn teach: How Great is the *Patience of God*; How Great is the *Power of God*, and How Great is the *Purpose of God.* There are four chapters in the Book of Jonah, and a careful examination of their content is necessary to understand the following headings. Chapter 1 describes *A Serious Decision,* Chapter 2 describes *A Striking Deliverance,* Chapter 3 speaks of *A Startling Declaration,* and the final chapter tells of *A Surprising Despondency.* The entire account explains how a very fine preacher went out of the will of God, became entangled in many perplexing problems, and finally how God restored His erring servant to a place of usefulness.

The place of prayer

"Now the Lord had prepared a great fish to swallow up Jonah." The word translated "fish" is the one that describes *a sea monster.* Many theologians consider this to have been a sea-dog or great shark. It should be remembered the white shark, often seen in Mediterranean waters, has been known to swallow humans and horses. History tells of a seaman who fell overboard and was swallowed by a fish. He was rescued when the whale was caught, and his strange testimony reminded the world of the experience known by Jonah. The possibility exists that God summoned one of these sea monsters to do His bidding, but on the other hand He could have created a special mammal to be the mini-submarine in which the runaway preacher was safely returned to land. How the task was performed is of secondary importance. Christians believe God holds the world in the hollow of His hand.

The Bible describes many places in which prayer was made, but the strangest was the stomach of this large fish. Imprisoned within this mammal yet remaining alive, Jonah realized his inability to outrun God. He probably began to consider three things: (1) God could have *punished him* for his flagrant disobedience. (2) God could have *pursued him*, and this obviously had been the case. (3) God could *exercise patience* with the stubborn man; and, since this too had taken place, it became obvious God had not rejected His servant. The Almighty, through the strange events that had taken place, was performing a miracle to return Jonah to his abandoned task. When Jonah realized these truths, the stomach of the fish became a temple; the captive began to pray.

The penitent plea

"When my soul fainted within me I remembered the LORD: and my prayer came in unto thee, into thine holy temple." Anything is possible when a man stops *running* and begins to *rest*! As Jonah considered his predicament, he said, "I am cast out of thy sight; yet I will look again toward thy holy temple." The prayer that followed indicated it was arising from a penitent soul. Yet of more importance to readers is the question: "*Did Jonah die?*" Afterward the prophet exclaimed: "Out of the belly of hell cried I, and thou heardest my voice." Hades, or Sheol, was the resting place of the dead, hence the translation "Out of the grave cried I." If Jonah prayed from Hell or Hades, then he was among the departed souls who had died. On the other hand, the prophet might have used the term because to all intent and purpose he was as good as dead! If Jonah had temporarily left this world, his experience would give added importance to the statement of the Lord recorded in Matthew 12:40: "For as Jonas was three days and three nights in the whale's belly; so shall the Son of man be three days and three nights in the heart of the earth." Jonah was a true type of Christ; his resurrection was a foreshadowing of the Lord's triumph over death.

The potent promise

"*BUT* I will sacrifice unto thee with the voice of thanksgiving; I will pay that that I have vowed. Salvation is of the LORD" (v. 9). Here we find one of those marvelously suggestive *buts* which represent "a turn in the road." Jonah had reached the end of his flight. He had wasted money on a voyage that was never completed, but he was given free transportation to his departure point. His statement regarding the observance of his vows indicates a change of attitude; the runaway was now willing to obey God and do what had to be done. At that moment, he was on his way home! "And the Lord spake unto the fish, and it vomited out Jonah upon the dry land" (v. 10). It has been ascertained that the whale, and perhaps all other great mammals of the sea, prior to death, vomit the contents of their stomachs. It is also a known fact that for some strange reason, whales sometimes come ashore to die. When these creatures are stranded on a beach, efforts are often made to return them to the sea, but they frequently refuse to cooperate with their human friends. They swim back to the shallow water, apparently preferring death to life. This might have been the reason that the great fish vomited out Jonah upon the dry land. This story suggests that the fish came into being to do the will of God. Throughout its lifetime, it never deviated from that pattern and, when it had been faithful unto death, it was content to die! Apparently it was wiser than men!

JONAH . . . the most phenomenal evangelist of all time (JONAH 3)

"And the word of the LORD came to Jonah *the second time* saying, Arise, go unto Nineveh, that great city, and preach unto it the preaching that I bid thee. So Jonah arose, and went unto Nineveh." Happy is the man who gets a second chance! The undeserving preacher was given the opportunity to make amends for his earlier failure.

A great city

Nineveh was a great city measuring nine miles in circumference. There were three other cities, which might be called suburbs of the metropolis. They were Rehoboth, Calon, and Resen, and all lay a half mile east of the Tigris River. Nineveh was built on a very lavish scale by Sennacherib, who had special pride in its features. The city had a library of several thousand clay tablets, a water channel which extended for thirty miles, a tremendous palace, and an encircling wall which gave adequate protection to the city. Archeologists have ascertained from unearthed tablets that the city of Calon, or Calah, one half the size of Nineveh, had a population of 69,754 people. This figure supports the fact that the entire district could easily have had 120,000 children. (See 4:11.) It has been estimated that to travel across the entire area would have taken three days. (See 3:3.) To go from one end of Nineveh to the city center would take one day. (See 3:4.)

From the edge of the sea, where the great fish deposited Jonah, to Nineveh, was a distance of over 600 miles. It has also been proved that an Arabian racing camel could travel one hundred miles per day. Jonah, having purchased or rented a camel, could have reached his destination within ten days even when allowing for rest periods. What followed his preaching beggared description.

A grievous concern

Jonah, having traveled across 600 miles of inhospitable wilderness, arrived at the edge of the great city and, having dismounted, led his camel through one of the fifteen gates and within moments commenced his strange sermon. Historical records attest to the fact that the area had already been devastated by two major earthquakes, so it may be safely assumed the people had been prepared for Jonah's arrival. The citizens were frightened; any thought of enduring further troubles filled them with dread. Yet the extent of the contrition — from the king to the slaves in the fields — presents problems. Why was Jonah so successful as a preacher? It would appear that within hours everybody in that part of the world was kneeling to ask God for forgiveness. Even the animals in the field had been covered with sackcloth and ashes. Every preacher in today's world would give everything he possesses if his ministry could be honored with such success.

There is reason to believe that Jonah's appearance did more than his utterances in bringing the Ninevites to their knees. He probably bore upon his body the slimy marks of his incarceration; and, since the Ninevites worshiped the Fish-God, they considered Jonah to be someone sent back from the grave to warn of impending destruction.

A glorious confession

"So the people of Nineveh believed God, and proclaimed a fast, and put on sackcloth . . . and [the king] arose from his throne, and he laid his robe from him, and covered him with sackcloth, and sat in ashes. And . . . caused it to be . . . published. . . . Who can tell if God will turn and repent, and turn away from his fierce anger, that we perish not?" Even Jonah was surprised by the electrifying results of his preaching. Soon, there was no need to repeat his prediction. His job was finished; he could have returned home immediately! As far as is known he was the first Jewish preacher to evangelize a gentile city; Jonah seemed to be a New Testament evangelist preaching to gentile listeners in an Old Testament age. Even then God was endeavoring to teach that His love encompassed the entire world and not just a select part of its inhabitants.

"And God saw their works, that they turned from their evil way; and God repented of the evil, that he had said that he would do unto them; and he did it not." Soon, everyone was smiling. God had relented; forgiveness was assured; the city was safe. Everyone was delighted except Jonah, whose face became overshadowed. He was disturbed and very annoyed. He was disgusted with his God and was ready to say so. In those moments Jonah once again disagreed with his Maker. When he went to the east side of the city to sit in the booth which his resolute hands erected, he was very angry. Alas, Jonah had cataracts on both his eyes!

JONAH . . . who did not appreciate success

(JONAH 4)

This is the bewildering story of an evangelist who did not want converts. Jonah was one of a type; there has never been another preacher like him. The first chapter described *Jonah Perishing* and we considered his *Brave Disobedience.* The second chapter told of *Jonah Praying* and we recognized his *Belated Decision.* The third chapter revealed *Jonah Preaching* and we admired his *Bold Declaration.* The fourth chapter tells of *Jonah Pouting,* and we are amazed to consider his *Bewildering Despair.* These simple headings enable students to understand the message contained in this remarkable book. Dismayed by the kindness of God in sparing the Ninevites, Jonah reminded the Lord how he had predicted what would take place. Recognizing the fact that the Ninevites were planning to invade Israel, he feared for the future of his nation. Jonah was correct. Fifty years later, Israel was devastated and appalled by the excessive cruelty of the heathens. Yet even in the lifetime of Jonah God was endeavoring to teach that He loved everybody. It should be remembered that this message had never been proclaimed; it was totally new. Gentiles were considered to be unclean; they were no better than scavengers!

God is reminded!

Jonah said, "I told You so, and You would not listen." "And he prayed unto the LORD, and said. . . . was not this my saying, when I was yet in my country? Therefore I fled before unto Tarshish: for I knew that thou art a gracious God, and merciful, slow to anger, and of great kindness, and repentest thee of the evil. Therefore now, O LORD, take, I pray thee, my life from me; for it is better for me to die than to live." Jonah's conception of the overwhelming mercy of God is unequaled in Old Testament writings. He knew that a cry for forgiveness would reach the heart of the Almighty but, alas, did not trust the sincerity of the Ninevites. Even should they be converted, their descendants would become the murderers of Israel. Jonah believed that prevention was better than cure; better that the parents should die before they gave birth to a race of merciless persecutors who would destroy innocent Hebrews. Jonah seemed to say, "God, I told You so; I knew what would happen, but You would not listen to me. I am no longer any use to Your people or myself. So please let me die." The *PREPARED THINGS* mentioned in the Book of Jonah suggest that God was equal to every emergency. He has not lost that ability.

God is responsive!

"Then said the LORD, Doest thou well to be angry?" Jonah's sun had been eclipsed by his cloudy problems. His vision had become impaired; he was unable to see beyond his disappointment. Utterly weary, he sat on the east side of the city to see what would happen. Maybe, so he thought, God will see the folly of His ways and destroy Nineveh after all! Then God prepared a gourd, a worm, and an east wind, and together these became the communication line between the miserable prophet and the overflowing heart of the Almighty. We have not been told much about the prophet's reactions, but it appears to be incongruous that a plant, a small creature, and a rushing wind should be better servants of God than an ordained preacher! Jonah resembled an automobile that had left the main highway to become bogged down in sand; Jonah was a bird with damaged wings, a well that had lost all its refreshing water. He loved his people so much that he forgot, temporarily, to trust God. It is wise to remember that, when any thing, or person, dethrones God in the affections of His people, there is danger! It is so easy for man to destroy himself, but it is impossible for a man to destroy the love of God which surrounds him.

God is right!

At first glance it might appear as though Jonah were right in his assessment of the situation. The Ninevites did destroy Israel, but there were other details to be considered. When God refused to destroy the city of Nineveh, He preserved a whole generation from destruction. At the same time, He was giving forty years in which Israel had the opportunity to repent of its own sins. When Jonah's beloved nation failed to respond to the message of contemporary prophets and when the people erected idols and deliberately worshiped them, they became as guilty as the Ninevites and deserved the punishment that befell them. The entire record teaches that God knew exactly what He was doing. Please read the later notes: "Nahum, the prophet Jonah would have loved."

We are not aware of the final reactions of the prophet, but at least we understand how Jonah would have appreciated the words of Paul who said: "I have great heaviness and continual sorrow in my heart. For I could wish that myself were accursed from Christ for my brethren, my kinsmen according to the flesh" (Rom. 9:2-3). Moses also expressed similar sentiments when he said: "Oh, this people have sinned a great sin. . . . Yet now, if thou wilt, forgive their sin — ; and if not, blot me, I pray thee, out of thy book which thou hast written" (Exod. 32:31-32). To love God is to love His children. A man without love is a tinkling cymbal. It would be interesting if we could decide which was the more effective, Jonah's heart or his head!

MICAH . . . who did not like prostitution

It is necessary to understand the period of time in which this man preached in Israel. The first verse in the book says he ministered "In the days of Jotham, Ahaz, and Hezekiah." The earlier kings had permitted idolatry and had encouraged forbidden practices. Hezekiah detested these things and tried to introduce spiritual reforms throughout the nation. He enjoyed partial success, but unfortunately the nobles and merchants did not cooperate. They agreed with the king but proceeded to do as they had always done. Micah came on the scene during this period and immediately denounced what he saw. He preached in the eighth century before Christ and was specially blessed by God.

The commissioning of Micah

The name given to this prophet was common throughout Israel; other men with the same name are mentioned in the Scriptures. Yet none was as outstanding as the one commissioned to preach. It is claimed that the name meant, "Who is like Jehovah?" and this indicates his parents were devout people. Not much can be authentically stated about him, but from his writings it may be deduced he came from Judaea and often preached around Jerusalem. His outspoken remarks were a terrible indictment of the priests, rulers, and merchants of his time. "And all the graven images thereof shall be beaten to pieces, and all the hires thereof shall be burned with fire, and all the idols thereof will I lay desolate: for *she gathered it of the hire of an harlot, and they shall return to the hire of an harlot"* (1:7). Israel had married prostitution to religious causes and thus set the abominable example still seen around the world. Exploiting the baser passions of lustful men, the priests sponsored houses of prostitution where sinners paid high fees for their pleasure. This practice provided the priests with a lavish income, some of which they doubtless retained. When Micah realized what was being done in the name of religion, his anger knew no limitations. He said, "Her wound is incurable" (1:9).

The coming of the Messiah

Micah saw the rising sun against this dark background! After a night of unprecedented gloom, the prophet saw a ray of hope and began to speak immortal words. "But thou, Bethlehem Ephratah, though thou be little among the thousands of Judah, yet out of thee shall he come forth unto me that is to be ruler in Israel; whose goings forth have been from of old, from everlasting" (5:2). It should be remembered that, although much of Micah's message was unacceptable to the religious leaders of the nation, these special words were never forgotten. Centuries later when the wise men asked where Christ should be born, Herod sought information regarding the predicted birthplace. "And [the chief priests and scribes of the people] said unto him, In Bethlehem of Judaea: for thus it is written by the prophet, And thou Bethlehem, in the land of Judah, art not the least among the princes of Judah: for out of thee shall come a Governor, that shall rule my people Israel" (Matt. 2:4-6). The fact that these men knew the truth and ultimately rejected it will be their greatest condemnation. The description stating "whose goings forth have been from of old, from everlasting" takes our thoughts back to eternity where the Lord shared fellowship within the Divine family. "In the beginning was the Word, and the Word was with God, and the Word was God" (John 1:1). Micah was disgusted with the sinfulness prevalent in his generation but was probably thrilled to announce the impending triumph of the Messiah.

The concern of the messenger

To read carefully the chapters of Micah's book is to see a very dark sky; yet to look more intently is to discover that frequently through the chapters stars shone amid the darkness of the heavens. Micah described both the wickedness of the nation and the judgments to be poured from God's presence. Nevertheless, here and there he reminded listeners of the compassionate nature of Jehovah. Perhaps his most wonderful utterance comes at the end of his book. "Who is a God like unto thee, that pardoneth iniquity, and passeth by the transgression of the remnant of his heritage? he retaineth not his anger for ever, because he delighteth in mercy" (7:18).

It is very doubtful whether any prophet, preacher, or pastor could fail to recognize the surpassing excellence of Micah's message. Obviously he was thrilled to describe the matchless mercy of God. To look into the face of Jesus is to explore the heart of the Almighty; to feel the support of His eternal arms is to be assured God's love is unchanging; it is from everlasting to everlasting.

NAHUM . . . the prophet Jonah would have loved

It is interesting to know that within the Greek Bible the Book of Nahum follows immediately after the book of Jonah. Actually it is the continuation of the story of the runaway prophet. Jonah was upset because he desired the total destruction of the Ninevites, and became rebellious when God spared the city. Fifty years later Nahum confronted the invading Ninevites and was thrilled to predict their doom. Three areas of thought invite investigation.

A city forgiven

Nahum in his introductory chapter spoke of *God's Power; God's Pity,* and *God's Purpose.* All these were exhibited in the saving of the city of Nineveh. Alas, the repentant sinners quickly forgot their vows, and their excessive cruelty beggared description. Monuments and tablets testify that they impaled prisoners alive; then whipped and beheaded them. Captives were dragged to death by ropes threaded through their lips. They were blinded by the king's own hand. They were hung up by hands or feet, and subjected to slow torture. Brains were beaten out, and tongues dragged out by the roots. It was a very sad day when these ferocious enemies invaded Israel and proceeded to torture Hebrew captives. Had Jonah been alive, he would have shouted for God to hear, "I told You this would happen, and You would not listen to me!" However, Jonah's successor was present to meet the invading enemies, and Nahum courageously denounced the atrocities of the Ninevites. It seems strange that he escaped unharmed. One would have expected the brutal enemies to silence forever this undaunted Hebrew prophet. Probably he survived because it was impossible to kill what God desired to remain alive.

A city forgetting

It is obvious that the Ninevites, who had professed repentance, returned to their evil ways. Their conversion did not last! Nahum, who ministered between seventy and eighty years after Jonah's preaching, was aware of the backsliding of the heathens, and with God-given courage proceeded to denounce them. He realized the strength of the enemy fortress but was adamant in his prediction that Nineveh would fall, that its citizens would reap what they had sown. Two things stand out in bold relief. *The Grace of God* relenting, and the *guilt of men* resisting. It is better not to make vows than to make them and then break them. Unless men will be accountable to God, there is no justice in law. Sinners may appear to triumph for a season, but ultimately the wrath of God falls upon the impenitent. The genuineness of true contrition is proved only by its longevity. This truth applies in any age and should be a deterrent when blasphemers insist God no longer exists. Someone has said, "The wheels of God grind slowly, but they grind exceeding small." To be caught in the teeth of those grinding, turning wheels of judgment is the greatest tragedy of all time.

A city falling

King Sennacherib had built an amazing city. It had fifteen ornate entrances, and the high walls were so impregnable that enemies considered Nineveh to be indestructible. God thought otherwise. History supplies accurate records of the destruction that swept Nineveh from its foundations. Torrential rain turned the Tigris into a raging, rolling body of irresistible water; the river overflowed its banks; and the unprecedented flood swept upon the city of Nineveh, dissolving the foundations and undermining its walls. And within a short period of time the once impregnable city was swept away like children's castles on a sandy beach. Surrounding nations might have asked, "How hath the mighty fallen?" but it became obvious that God endorsed what the prophet had said. "Behold, I am against thee, saith the LORD of hosts; and I will discover thy skirts upon thy face, and I will show the nations thy nakedness, and the kingdoms thy shame. And I will cast abominable filth upon thee, and make thee vile, and will set thee as a gazingstock. And it shall come to pass that all they that look upon thee shall flee from thee, and say, Nineveh is laid waste: who will bemoan her?" (3:5-7). The man or nation who forgets or fights against God eloquently advertises stupidity. It is infinitely better to have God as a friend than a foe.

It becomes evident that even in the earliest days of civilization God was stamping upon the conscience of mankind the necessity for righteousness and mercy, the recognition of evil and holiness. It remains a cause for regret that modern people appear to be as indifferent as their forefathers. Yet the message of God remains unchanged. "For if we sin wilfully after that we have received the knowledge of the truth, there remaineth no more sacrifice for sins, But a certain fearful looking for of judgment and fiery indignation, which shall devour the adversaries" (Heb. 10:26-27). Only fools sleep when a prophet is speaking!

HABAKKUK . . . the mockingbird prophet

There are only three chapters in this little-known Old Testament book, but all who wish to acquire an understanding of Habakkuk's message should read carefully the entire book. The chief characteristic of a mockingbird is its ability to sing through the darkest night. The conditions mentioned in these chapters were very depressing, but to appreciate the reasons for the difficult times, it is necessary to read 2 Chronicles 33:1-13. This prophet ministered during the reign of Manasseh, whose terrible example led Israel into sin and captivity. The enemies were permitted by God to invade Israel and enslave its citizens. The scintillating splendor of the nation was completely destroyed, and the havoc that followed surpassed anything known in the experiences of the nation. Habakkuk ministered during the dreadful days that preceded the storm.

CHAPTER 1 . . . *The man who prayed*

It would appear as if an ancient technician tape-recorded a conversation between the prophet and his God. It is necessary to read the chapter slowly and to note where Habakkuk ceased praying and began listening. He knew that prayer was a two-way affair; a telephone to heaven; a line used at both ends! Habakkuk prayed and then listened, and it is easy to identify these distinctions in the midst of the recorded statements. A saint who does all the asking and never listens exhibits selfishness. The saint who does all listening and never asks God for anything cannot rejoice over answered prayer. He gets what he asks — nothing! James said, "Ye have not, because ye ask not" (James 4:2). This prophet had difficulty understanding why God was slow in handling matters of urgency. "Art thou not from everlasting, O LORD my God, mine Holy One? . . . wherefore lookest thou upon them that deal treacherously, and holdest thy tongue when the wicked devoureth the man that is more righteous than he?" He seemed to be saying, "O Lord, the sinners are prospering here; the righteous are suffering, and You, O Lord, do nothing!" Habakkuk's ideas never died; his questions are still being asked.

CHAPTER 2 . . . *The man who preached*

The statement "Woe unto him" appeared to be the main thrust of the prophet's message; he could not expect to become popular. He was a very ominous cloud in what otherwise would have been a blue sky. The idol makers, the wine makers, and others of their type were becoming wealthy. Financiers thought only of their wealth; hypocrites cared nothing for the prohibitions of law; they did what they pleased. Habakkuk saw this and became infuriated. His "Woes" were meant to strike terror into the hearts of listeners. Sometimes it is hard to explain how men of his type disappeared! This strange but wonderful prophet never lost sight of God. He exclaimed: "But the LORD is in his holy temple: let all the earth keep silence before him" (2:20). Many events baffled the mind of the preacher; the ways of God were beyond comprehension; and yet, so Habakkuk insisted, God knew what He was doing.

CHAPTER 3 . . . *The man who perceived*

Writing his third chapter, the preacher contrasted the majesty of God with the misery of men, and the resultant conclusion filled him with concern. He realized the forthcoming experiences of Israel would be frightening and depressing, but, as a mockingbird, he sang through the gloom. Then suddenly a bright and glorious morning began to dispel the darkness. He wrote: "Although the fig tree shall not blossom, neither shall fruit be in the vines; the labour of the olive shall fail, and the fields shall yield no meat; the flock shall be cut off from the fold, and there shall be no herd in the stalls; Yet I will rejoice in the LORD, I will joy in the God of my salvation. The LORD God is my strength" (3:17-19). That Habakkuk was a musician seems obvious, because he dedicated his book to the chief singer of "my stringed instruments." This remarkable prophet seemed to know that, although sorrow endured for a night, joy came in the morning! Storms might threaten Israel, but the Almighty held the elements in His hands and, as long as He loved His people, their destiny remained assured and safe. The message from this ancient preacher is still potent. Maybe the poet realized this when he wrote:

Days of darkness still come o'er me;
Sorrow's path I sometimes tread;
But the Savior still is with me,
By His hand I'm safely led.

Good music in the darkness is better than loud noises disturbing the day. Happy is the singer whose songs are never silenced by sorrow.

ZEPHANIAH . . . who became angry in a hurry

There are three chapters in this strange book; they should be studied carefully. At first there seems to be little connection between them; the prophet was very disturbed. Zephaniah was of royal descent from King Hezekiah, by whom certain reforms had been instituted in Judah. He ministered about 600 years before Christ, but, when he commenced preaching, he was angry. He was so disgusted with what he saw that he pronounced judgment against everybody. Reforms ordered by Hezekiah had only been partially carried out; the country was still littered with idols; the rulers exploited their people; hypocrisy was everywhere. To understand these features is to know why the prophet was incensed.

CHAPTER 1 . . . *The condemnation of the people*

Zephaniah began by denouncing Israel, who knew the law but ignored its commandments. The prophet, seeing the terrible things taking place in the cities and towns of Israel, commenced to predict overwhelming disaster on people who blatantly worshiped idols. He predicted God would use heathens to chastise the Hebrews, and that afterward even they would be punished for "touching the apple of God's eye." He mentioned in 1:6-8 (1) *The Lord's people*; (2) *The Lord's presence*; (3) *the Lord's sacrifice.* It is interesting to note how many times he referred to "the day of the Lord." He was acutely aware that God was angry with the abominable practices in Israel and that He would permit catastrophies to overwhelm His people. Their enemies would overrun the country, self-confidence would be destroyed, and those who believed God "did not care" would suddenly discover their preconceived ideas were wrong. The prophet said: "The great day of the LORD is near, it is near, and hasteth greatly, even the voice of the day of the LORD; the mighty man shall cry there bitterly. That day is a day of wrath, a day of trouble and distress, a day of wasteness and desolation, a day of darkness and gloominess, a day of clouds and thick darkness" (1:14-15). That all these predictions were fulfilled should remind everybody that God meant what He said.

CHAPTER 2 . . . *The consolation of the penitent*

It is thrilling to detect that against the somber darkness of the prophet's sky, stars of encouragement began to appear. Having denounced wickedness, Zephaniah said: "Seek ye the LORD, all ye meek of the earth . . . it may be ye shall be hid in the day of the LORD'S anger . . . for the remnant of the house of Judah . . . shall lie down in the evening; for the LORD their God shall visit them, and turn away their captivity" (2:3,7). Even in His anger, the Lord would be gracious. When judgment devastated the land, there would always be a hiding place for those who sought it. Zephaniah preached amid the blackness of Israel's night, but he was aware of a glorious dawn beginning to appear in the eastern sky. He predicted enemies would overrun the land, but after the Babylonian captivity things would change; Israel would return home. God's grace is always greater than man's sin.

CHAPTER 3 . . . *The consummation of the promise*

The predictions of the prophet in his final chapter suggests important questions. Zephaniah was certainly thinking about the post-Babylonian period, but some of his statements were not fulfilled at that time. He said: "The remnant of Israel shall not do iniquity . . . . Sing, O daughter of Zion; shout, O Israel; be glad and rejoice with all the heart, O daughter of Jerusalem. The LORD hath taken away thy judgments; he hath cast out thine enemy: *the king of Israel, even the LORD, is in the midst of thee: thou shalt not see evil any more*" (3:13-15). Those predictions were never fulfilled, and that encourages the belief that Zephaniah was speaking of the last days when Christ will reign over His people. Only then could the prophet's words apply. "The LORD thy God in the midst of thee is mighty; he will save, he will rejoice over thee with joy; he will rest in his love, he will joy over thee with singing . . . . At that time will I bring you again, even in the time that I gather you: for I will make you a name and a praise among all the people of the earth" (3:17-20).

To obtain an understanding of the intensity of God's purpose and the extent of His love, it is necessary to compare and contrast the beginning and the end of this Book of Zephaniah. It is possible to recognize veiled foreshadowings of the salvation that saves from the guttermost to the uttermost. The God who lifts people from the depths of sinful degradation continues to lift them until they are clothed with resplendent beauty. Probably, in all its ramifications, God's grace is too great for finite minds to comprehend.

HAGGAI . . . and his revival crusade

It is interesting to read both chapters of this strange little book and to notice the dates that are mentioned. This prophet made his appearance almost a hundred years after the Babylonian captivity. Many things had influenced Haggai when he began to preach to decadent people. Cyrus, the leader of the Medo-Persians, had released the captives from Babylon, and these, under the guidance of Nehemiah and Ezra, returned to their devastated country to reconstruct Jerusalem. At first the enthusiasm was overwhelming, but as time passed the early fervor began to wane. Haggai was used by God to rekindle the old desires and send the Jews back to the forsaken tasks.

The sixth month . . . the sixth day (Hag. 1:1)

"The word of the LORD by Haggai the prophet. . . . Thus speaketh the LORD of hosts, saying, This people say, The time is not come, the time that the LORD'S house should be built. . . . Is it time for you, O ye, to dwell in your ceiled houses, and this house lie waste? Now therefore saith the LORD of hosts, *Consider your ways*" (vv. 1-5). God had always said in one way or another: "Seek ye first the kingdom of God, and his righteousness, and all [other] things shall be added unto you" (Matt. 6:33). The people of Israel had reversed the order. They had built their homes, and were living comfortably. Complacency gripped their souls, and they resisted any suggestion that gave priority to the work of God. Their attitude said: "We have many things to do; we do not have time to devote to building the house of God. There is no hurry; that task can wait."

The sixth month . . . the twenty-fourth day (Hag. 1:14)

The prophet continued his preaching for eighteen days, and his task was difficult. Then, "The LORD stirred up the spirit of Zerubbabel the son of Shealtiel governor of Judah, and the spirit of Joshua the son of Josedech, the high priest, and the spirit of all the remnant of the people, and they came and did work in the house of the LORD of hosts, their God" (1:14). What might have happened if the preacher had grown weary after eight or ten days? Every minister should realize he is "a worker *together with God.*" Although evidences of success may not at first appear, faith sees the Holy Spirit working in the hearts of listeners. No servant of God is ever justified in quitting his task unless God gives direct orders for him so to do. God commands us to be *faithful* unto death. It is providential that He did not say, "Be *successful* unto death." If that were the case, some of us could have retired before we began.

The seventh month . . . the twenty-first day (Hag. 2:1-3)

"In the seventh month, in the one and twentieth day of the month, came the word of the LORD by the prophet Haggai, saying . . . Who is left among you that saw this house in her first glory? and how do ye see it now? is it not in your eyes in comparison of it as nothing?" (vv. 1-3). Nearly a month had passed since the people returned to their task, but, alas, what was being done was far from satisfactory. Were the people slow? Were they careless, not giving attention to details? We do not know, but their efforts left much to be desired. Then God said, "Be strong, all ye people of the land, saith the LORD, *and work*: for I am with you, saith the LORD of hosts" (2:4). The hand of the Lord was resting heavily upon Haggai, insomuch that, as we now study the content of his message, the question arises, "To which temple was he referring?" "The glory of this latter house shall be greater than of the former . . . and in this place will I give peace, saith the LORD of hosts" (2:9). Answers may vary, but obviously the blessing on man's labor is governed by the quality and dedication of what is done.

The ninth month . . . the twenty-fourth day (Hag. 2:10)

It is extremely thought-provoking to study the occasions when the prophet urged his listeners "to consider their ways." Self-examination is infinitely superior to a critical observation of others! Haggai drew attention to the decreasing harvests and emphasized the fact that the sanctification of everything pertaining to God's work was more important than the labor of the people. His indictment of the priests was frightening. His questioning revealed they had been careless in the acceptance of impure offerings, and as a result the entire nation had become unclean in the eyes of God. His closing statements remind of the hymn: "Grace, grace; God's grace; Grace that is greater than all our sin." It is stimulating to remember that God's grace lasts longer than His wrath!

ZECHARIAH . . . who was greatly informed

The prophets Zechariah and Haggai were contemporaries; they ministered to the same people. Either contributed to the other, but the contents of their books were very different. Haggai was the preacher; Zechariah, the poet. The former was a fiery evangelist; the second was a mystic, a seer whose vision scanned the ages. This book is the most important of the entire Minor Prophet collection. It stands alone in magnificence, and its author describes events not mentioned by any other minor prophet. The chapters divide into three categories.

His visions of mercy (Zech. 1-6)

Eight chapters in the book speak of the matchless mercy of Jehovah. They affirm that, although Israel seemed eternally lost, God intended to make the nation more wonderful than it had ever been. Chapter 2:8 states that Israel was the apple of God's eye, and it would be dangerous for any persecutor to harass the children of the most high God. The successive visions of the prophet told the same story; the greatest concept in the mind of Zechariah was the boundless mercy of God. Dealing with this theme, the prophet said God would send forth His special servant "the BRANCH," and all divine purposes would be centered in him. (See 3:8.) It is thrilling and profitable to study the visions of Zechariah, to make a list and compare every one with the other. God would never forsake His people; the long standing covenant with Abraham would be honored. God would not only bless Israel, but He would also bless all those who helped the chosen people.

His visions of mistakes (Zech. 5-7)

By comparing 1:1 with 7:1 it will be seen that two years had passed since Zechariah commenced his ministry. During that time progress had been made, but formality was threatening reality in the experiences of the nation. Though they apparently observed fasts and feasts and there was much ostentation, apparently people wept only to be seen and heard of others. They were not truly penitent. When appointed intercessors came to the temple to pray, they appeared to be part of an organized professional act. God, through the prophet, interrupted their devotions and said: "When ye fasted and mourned in the fifth and seventh month, even those seventy years, *did ye at all fast unto me, even to me*? And when ye did eat, and when ye did drink, *did not ye eat for yourselves, and drink for yourselves*? Should ye not hear the words which the LORD hath cried by the former prophets . . . ?" (7:5-7). Too much emphasis had been placed upon ritual, forms, and ceremonies; yet there were no tears, no contrition, and no devotion in their hearts. The prophet reminded everybody that a broken and contrite heart was more to be desired than offerings, that a man was never as tall as when he knelt before his Maker.

His visions of majesty (Zech. 9-14)

It is interesting to count the times Zechariah said: "And the word of the LORD came saying. . . ." It would appear that this unique prophet did more *listening* than *speaking*. When he preached, he prefaced all his remarks with "Thus saith the LORD," or, "The word of the LORD came unto me." Wise and blessed is the preacher who develops that habit! There are so many important Scriptures in the closing chapters of this book that it becomes difficult to know where to begin and where to cease. Referring to the country's two rainy seasons known as "the first and the latter rains," Zechariah said that, in addition to blessings already received, unprecedented showers of blessings would still come to Israel. Chapters 12-14 are among the most thrilling parts of the Scriptures.

Speaking of the ultimate triumph of the Hebrews, the prophet said: "In that day shall the LORD defend the inhabitants of Jerusalem" (12:8). "And they shall look upon me whom they have pierced" (12:10). "In that day there shall be a fountain opened . . . for sin and uncleanness" (13:1). "And one shall say unto him, What are these wounds in thine hands? Then he shall answer, Those with which I was wounded in the house of my friends" (13:6). "And his feet shall stand in that day upon the mount of Olives" (14:4). "And the LORD shall be king over all the earth: in that day shall there be one LORD, and his name one" (14:9). For a detailed explanation of these amazing verses, consult the author's book, *What in the World Will Happen Next?*

MALACHI . . . the last of the Old Testament prophets

In order to understand the conditions in which Malachi ministered, it is necessary to read Nehemiah 13:7. At the end of the Babylonian captivity, the Jews were permitted by King Cyrus to return to their homeland to reconstruct what had been devastated. Their leaders, Ezra and Nehemiah, were given letters of commendation to rulers along the way so that the people would not be molested, and furthermore, the authorities were commanded to supply materials needed for the restoration of Jerusalem. During the rebuilding, Nehemiah returned to Babylon to report to his sponsor. When he returned after a long absence, he was dismayed by the backslidden state of the people. Ezra was probably dead, heathens were living in the temple, and no one cared. The Book of Nehemiah describes the actions taken to rectify the situation, but the task became increasingly difficult. It was at this time God commissioned Malachi to support, strengthen, and encourage the national leader. His ministry became a light shining in the midst of the post-captivity apathy of Israel.

His perception

Malachi recorded for posterity what he saw. The people and the priests had become indifferent to the work of the Lord. They offered imperfect sacrifices and polluted bread. They gave to God what they did not value. No service was motivated by love, for every person connected with the temple demanded payment for everything done. He asked, "Who is there even among you that would shut the doors for nought? neither do ye kindle fire on mine altar for nought. I have no pleasure in you, saith the LORD of hosts, neither will I accept an offering at your hand" (1:10). The early gratitude known when the power of God broke the shackles of bondage and brought Israel out of Babylon had disappeared. The people were now concerned with getting, and not giving. They had a form of godliness, but no love for the Lord. It is easy to recognize the same symptoms among church people of our modern age.

His preaching

When this wonderful prophet compared the priests of his generation with those who ministered in earlier times, certain features became obvious: (1) *How Factual*; (2) *How Fearless*; (3) *How Frightening*. Malachi reminded the priests that God had made a covenant with Levi, their ancestor, in which He promised to bless faithful descendants. Malachi said: "The law of truth was in [Levi's] mouth. . . . But ye are departed out of the way" (2:6-8). The outstanding courage of this amazing preacher was evident when he said: ''Behold, I will corrupt your seed and spread dung upon your faces.'' Malachi obviously feared only God. This is the hallmark of a true prophet. Then he mentioned a very potent thing. The rulers of the nation had abandoned their wives in favor of other women. (See 2:14.) Their outward profession of loving service was only a sham; they pleased themselves, not God. If they did not repent, they would perish.

His predictions

''Behold, I will send my messenger, and he shall prepare the way before me: and the LORD, whom ye seek, shall suddenly come to his temple. . . . But who may abide the day of his coming? and who shall stand when he appeareth? for he is like a refiner's fire, and like fullers' soap'' (3:1-3). God's Messenger would come to *His* temple! No ordinary man could claim to be the owner of the temple of God! A refiner of silver exposed dross in molten metal. When God's Messiah came to His temple, He would reveal and expose everything hypocritical in those who professed to be righteous. They should beware; they were in danger!

His promises

Malachi was surely thrilled when he reminded his listeners that, in spite of all they had done, God could still be merciful. He could and would open the windows of heaven and pour out His blessing. (See 3:10.) The only prerequisite for revival was that they should obey the word of God, and bring their tithes into God's storehouse. We do not know how many of the listeners responded to Malachi's appeal, but some became part of a chosen fellowship. ''They that feared the LORD spake often one to another: and the LORD hearkened, and heard it, and a book of remembrance was written before him for them that feared the LORD, and that thought upon his name'' (3:16). This message is urgently needed today.

JESUS . . . amid the famous and foolish

(MATTHEW 2:1-16)

Sooner or later every person must be confronted by the claims of Christ, for it was destined He would become the center and circumference of everything. This became evident even at His birth.

The unforgettable scholars . . . inspired (Matt. 2:1-2)

Little is known about the illustrious men who traveled far in search of the infant king. Yet we are justified in assuming certain things, for they appear to be obvious. (1) They could not have been young men for they were skilled astronomers able to understand the movements of stars. When they saw a star of outstanding brilliance they correctly interpreted it as a sign that somewhere a new king had been born. (2) They could not have been peasants, for the wealthy gifts they brought to Jesus indicated they were affluent, and able to pay for what could only have been a very expensive journey. (3) They were wise and prudent with a real knowledge of God. They understood, appreciated, and obeyed every command given to them. They probably traveled great distances across the desert but, implicitly believing God was motivating the guiding star, followed faithfully until they were able to place their gifts at the feet of the royal Baby. They were very wise, and all wise people, both men and women, have emulated their noble example. They came to worship the Son of God.

The unforgivable schemer . . . incensed (Matt. 2:16)

Three details became outstanding in the reactions of King Herod. His fear, faith, and folly. The news of the birth of a king filled him with dread, and he became unreasonable. Even if the new Baby became a king, that would take at least another twenty years, and by that time Herod would probably be dead. Clear reasoning would have suggested that the Babe of Bethlehem could never have been a threat to Herod's personal prestige and power. The man was stupid! Nevertheless, he believed the Scriptures and asked the chief priest and the scribes to name the birthplace of the Messiah. Whether he was motivated by fear or faith, it may be hard to decide, but the desired information was soon forthcoming. To know the will of God and reject it is suicidal. To turn revelation into resistance is disastrous, and why Herod should do this is hard to comprehend. Thwarted by the wisdom of the wise men, Herod became incensed and commanded that all the infants around Bethlehem be slaughtered. He was a very great fool, as indeed are all men who fight against God.

The unconcerned scribes . . . indifferent (Matt. 2:5, 17-18)

Matthew was able to write: "Then was fulfilled that which was spoken by Jeremy the prophet, saying, In Rama was there a voice heard, lamentation, and weeping, and great mourning, Rachel weeping for her children, and would not be comforted, because they are not." Probably at that time, the scribes knew more about the statements of the prophets than any other people. They studied and copied the prophetic manuscripts and had correctly identified the Messiah's birthplace. Yet they who knew so much did nothing. Those men were the most difficult to understand. Apparently they had no need to search the Scriptures; they quoted from memory the prediction made by the prophet Micah. "And thou, Bethlehem, in the land of Judah, art not the least among the princes of Judah: for out of thee shall come a Governor, that shall rule my people Israel." (See Micah 5:2.) The subject was nationally important, and it would have been feasible that the scribes would at least have investigated the situation. Apparently they remained unconcerned when the cries of bereaved mothers rent the nation. They probably shrugged their shoulders and exclaimed, "It's none of our business." Their apathy was deplorable; their conduct, inexcusable. Their behavior enables readers of the gospel to understand why they were often called hypocrites. It might be very difficult to decide which type of man was the most despicable — Herod who knew the truth and resisted it or the scribe who also knew the truth but remained unconcerned.

Even before Jesus could walk or talk, He was the center of attraction even as He is today. Wise men still come to Him; unrepentant sinners still resist and hate Him. Perhaps the worst kind of people are they who ignore Him. He is nonexistent in their world, as they will be in His world. The statement "But when Herod was dead" provides a fitting epitaph for the king's tomb. He lost his throne, his life, and his soul, and for such a catastrophe there could never be compensation.

THE LORD . . . who often speaks in a storm

(MATTHEW 8:24; JONAH 1:4; ACTS 27:13-18)

Storms are never welcomed at sea or on land unless the earth has been parched by drought. Awesome beauty and majesty may be seen in the powers of nature when they are liberated in the heavens, but cyclones, tornadoes, and other storms are devastating when homes are destroyed and communities shattered. The same truth applies within the human spirit. Men and women desire peace and serenity; when stormy circumstances destroy the happiness of homes, laughter is turned to tears. There are occasions when it seems incomprehensible that God should permit storms to harass His people; it is even more difficult to understand why, sometimes, He plans them for the welfare of His children. The storms of the Bible are instructive; let us therefore examine three Scriptures supplied by ancient writers.

The disciples' storm . . . God's rescuing program . . . there is a presence

"And when he was entered into a ship, his disciples followed him. And, behold, there arose a great tempest in the sea, insomuch that the ship was covered with the waves: but he was asleep. And his disciples came to him, and awoke him, saying, Lord, save us: we perish" (Matt. 8:23-25). Those fishermen often encountered storms on the Sea of Galilee, but this occurrence was exceptional; the waves terrified them. When the disciples looked at their sleeping Master, they were filled with apprehension, for it seemed the boat was about to sink. Their desperate cry for assistance brought relief, but apparently the men failed to recognize that nothing could sink a ship in which Jesus was a passenger! He was with them in the storm, and was aware of their plight. As their Master and Friend, He was capable of being extremely tired, but there was another side of His nature which "never slumbered nor slept" (Ps. 121:1-4). Even a sleeping Christ was a better guarantee of safety than the most skillful pilot who remained awake!

Jonah's storm . . . God's restraining power . . . there is a pattern

Jonah, the prophet, was displeased with God; his soul was in rebellion. As far as he was concerned, the Lord could go to Nineveh and do His own preaching! He was getting out fast; he was quitting his job, and the decision was final. He had found a ship about to sail for Tarshish, and had paid his fare, and there was nothing God could do about the matter. He smiled and lay down to sleep, but his reasoning was out of alignment with the mind of the Almighty. Poor Jonah — his sleep became a nightmare. He was running away from God, but, alas, he ran too slowly! When eventually the seamen threw him overboard, the prophet probably smiled even more. The Lord had overtaken him on the ship but would be unable to take him from the waters of death. He was wrong again, for when Jonah was thrown into the sea, he fell into the everlasting arms of God's kindness. God loved the people of Nineveh, but He also loved Jonah; and, although the runaway prophet had turned his back on the Lord, Jehovah still had His face toward the errant prophet. It is wise to remember that forsaking God is no guarantee He forsakes us. He has ways and means of accomplishing within us that which we could never do for ourselves. This is the pattern of all His associations with undeserving people.

Paul's storm . . . God's reassuring promise . . . there is a peace

"And when neither sun nor stars in many days appeared, and no small tempest lay on us, all hope that we should be saved was then taken away" (Acts 27:20). Thus did Luke summarize the situation on a ship destined to sink. The Mediterranean Sea had become a raging tempest; no man could survive; they were doomed! "But after long abstinence Paul stood forth in the midst of them, and said . . . be of good cheer: for I believe God, that it shall be even as it was told me. Howbeit we must be cast upon a certain island" (Acts 27:20-26). Paul could not have known that a three-month evangelistic crusade had been planned by God and that his presence was urgently required, for a man named Publius, who lived on the island, was desperately ill and needed help. Had there been no storm to hasten the arrival of the ship, the sufferer would have died from continuing hemorrhaging, and many of the islanders would not have heard the gospel.

We do not know how much the Lord told His servant, but it became obvious, that after Paul had spoken with the Lord, his soul was filled with peace. He knew the storm had been planned by God, and in due time the reason would be disclosed. His testimony: "For there stood by me this night the angel of God, whose I am, and whom I serve, Saying, Fear not, Paul, thou must be brought before Caesar, and, lo, God hath given thee all them that sail with thee," revealed the amazing confidence he shared with his Maker. The threatening storm was an instrument in an omnipotent hand. The rough waves and shrieking winds were messengers of the Almighty. It is wise to remember that Paul's God is our God, and in His hand we are safe.

Master, the terror is over;
  The elements sweetly rest.
Earth's sun in the calm lake is mirrored,
  And heaven's within my breast.

THE LORD . . . and His unfailing promises

The promises of God are the most reliable things in the world. When He says, "I will," men may be assured He will never violate an agreement. Among nations important documents have to be read, studied, signed, and witnessed. Often great pressure has to be exerted on signatories to make them honor commitments, but with God this is never necessary. I once asked a diamond merchant if he ever had trouble with people who broke pledges. He gravely replied, "We never sign documents; when we shake hands on a deal, that is it! If a man violated an agreement, he would never again be trusted by his colleagues." Similarly, God's promise is His bond, and it is thrilling to discover the Bible contains many of the "I wills" of the Almighty.

"I will give you rest" (Matt. 11:28)

This promise of the Savior is one of the most outstanding of His utterances. No other person could have made such a claim. A millionaire might offer money; a wise man may offer advice. A man in an eminent position in industry could offer help to the unemployed, but no man can promise rest except Jesus. Rest is beyond the purchasing power of money; it is something that applies to man's deepest need. It is an elusive treasure only found at Christ's feet. It is significant that, although two thousand years have passed since Jesus made the promise and although millions of people have responded, no person ever came in vain. The Lord had no money but has enriched the lives of kings and queens. He never attended a university, but the libraries of the world are filled with books about Him. He never had an army; yet His followers have conquered nations without fighting. Jesus substituted love for force and tenderness for weapons, and His methods never failed. He invited people to come, and those who did were satisfied.

"I will not fail thee, nor forsake thee" (Josh. 1:5)

When Joshua succeeded Moses and became the leader of Israel, he was confronted with a monumental task. The Canaanites had to be subdued, the criticism of Israel silenced, and innumerable problems solved. Although Joshua had been trained by Moses, the fact remained the younger man did not possess the knowledge and experience of the patriarch, who had brought the nation out of Egypt. Yet, he undertook to do the will of God and triumphed magnificently. Undoubtedly his success was outstanding because he relied upon the promises of God. He had been told, "There shall not any man be able to stand before thee all the days of thy life; as I was with Moses, so *I will be with thee.*" It is refreshing to know that

God makes the same promise to all who journey toward the Promised Land. Christians need not fight battles alone. God, who called and commissioned His followers, promised to be with them always. The saint is assured of excellent company as he proceeds toward his eternal home.

"I will repay thee" (Luke 10:35)

When the Savior told the parable of the Good Samaritan, He enshrined within it immortal truths. Doubtless He meant to infer He was the great Benefactor who found the suffering man alongside the path of life. His grace met the man's need, and His thoughtfulness prepared for the victim's future. He "set him on his own beast, and brought him to an inn, and took care of him. And on the morrow when he departed, he took out two pence, and gave them to the host, and said unto him, Take care of him; and whatsoever thou spendest more, when I come again, *I will repay thee.*" (See Luke 10:33-35.) The innkeeper may be likened to the church or any person who cares for converts. To assist people is to do the will of the Savior. What is conscientiously done for Him will be rewarded when Christ returns to earth. No man can outgive God; He knows how to compensate His children.

"I will come again" (John 14:3)

Prior to His departure from earth, Jesus addressed the disciples and said, "I go to prepare a place for you. And if I go and prepare a place for you, *I will come again,* and receive you unto myself; that where I am, there ye may be also" (John 14:3). That was possibly the most important of all His promises. Even in the earliest days of church history when saints became martyrs, inspiration was gleaned from the fact that either they would go to Him or He would come to them. Death no longer terrified them; they were able to exclaim, "O death, where is thy sting? O grave, where is thy victory?" To those inspired Christians, the grave was but an underground tunnel leading to the celestial city. They were able to repeat the words of David, "Yea, though I walk through the valley of the shadow of death, I will fear no evil: for thou art with me" (Ps. 23:4). If they died, they did so triumphantly; if they lived, they looked for His personal return. They believed He meant what He said. That has been the inspiration of the church in all ages, and it constantly thrills those who believe the Bible. Many indications of Christ's return may be seen today; there is reason to believe this age is drawing to conclusion.

God is working His purpose out
  As year succeeds to year.
God is working His purpose out,
  And the time is drawing near.

THE MERCHANT . . . who bought a pearl of great price (MATTHEW 13:45-46)

This word picture was easily understood by the Lord's listeners; pearls were in great demand throughout the ancient world. Cultured pearls were unknown in antiquity and any kind of pearl was considered to be of great value. These treasures were constantly sought by peddlers who were assured of great profits when they resold their gems. Nevertheless, this parable was of tremendous interest because of the words used by Jesus. This seeker after pearls was no mere peddler.

The meticulous person

Jesus spoke of a "merchant man, seeking goodly pearls." According to Dr. Thayer, there were two important words used in this connection. The first was *emporos* which implied "a collector" or "a dealer of great wealth." This was no ordinary street peddler nor even a retailer. He was a wealthy man, possibly a collector of rare gems. The same word is used in Revelation 18:23 where the merchants (*emporoi*) are said to be "the great men of the earth." The second word used was *kapeelos* which meant "a peddler; a dealer; a retailer." The picture thus provided was not that of a money-making dealer but of a skilled connoisseur, a collector of rare gems with an almost inexhaustible supply of purchasing power.

This has been the one parable about which all theologians agree. The pearl of great price is the church formed through suffering. The man said to be seeking the treasure is Christ, the Son of God and the Prince of heaven. Dr. Thayer further states the word *emporos* was used in ancient writings to indicate a man who goes "on a journey, whether by sea or by land, especially for traffic or business." This, of course, was in harmony with the theme of the parable. The Prince of heaven came to earth to search for and to acquire something of tremendous value. "He sacrificed all that He had" to obtain His pearl.

The magnificent pearl

It should be noted that the seeker was looking for "goodly" pearls. The Greek word used here is *kalous* which means, "beautiful, handsome, excellent, eminent, choice, surpassing, precious, suitable, commendable, admirable, beautiful to look at, shapely, magnificent." *Kalous* is no ordinary word. The seeker was only interested in gems of surpassing excellence. That he only found *one* pearl embodying all these qualities provides food for thought. Pearls are formed through suffering. A small grain of irritating sand creates pain inside the shell of an oyster. The mollusc, "upon this grain of sand, deposits a thin crust of brilliant material. How often this is repeated, no one can tell; one deposit after another is made till at last in the side of the oyster, there is found a most beautiful pearl, a pearl of great price, a pearl in which the colors of the rainbow of the heavens are wonderfully blended together. It is taken up and becomes the well nigh priceless jewel in the crown of some mighty monarch" (Arno C. Gaebelein. *The Gospel of Matthew;* p. 300). The pearl of great price can only be the church created through the sufferings of the Savior. There could only be *one* of this type.

The memorable price

The special collector, as suggested by the Greek word, had to be exceedingly wealthy, but the added detail that "he sold all that he had" therefore suggests great sacrifice. In modern language, the multimillionaire became penniless through one tremendous transaction. Basically, he had nothing left except the acquired pearl, but he obviously considered the purchase worthwhile. There can be no way to measure the love with which he looked at His gem. The Prince of heaven, "Who, being in the form of God, thought it not robbery to be equal with God: But made himself of no reputation, and took upon him the form of a servant, and was made in the likeness of men: And being found in fashion as a man, he humbled himself, and became obedient unto death, even the death of the cross" (Phil. 2:6-8). The seeker after the pearl of great price literally gave all that He had — even His life, but obviously He thought it worthwhile — how greatly Jesus must have loved us!

The matchless pleasure

It is difficult to understand completely the Lord's satisfaction in purchasing the church. Maybe the nearest we can approach to that superlative appreciation is to remember how ten thousand times ten thousand and thousands of thousands will sing, "Thou art worthy . . . for thou wast slain, and hast redeemed us to God by thy blood, out of every kindred, and tongue, and people, and nation; And hast made us unto our God kings and priests: and we shall reign on the earth" (Rev. 5:9-10). When the Lord Jesus listens to the anthem of His redeemed choir, He will be thrilled, and perhaps might borrow our language and exclaim, "*It was worth it all*" (Condensed from the author's commentary, *Matthew's Majestic Gospel*, pp. 262-264).

FOUR FACES OF JESUS . . . and their changing expressions

If I were an artist, I would paint a portrait of the Lord, but I am sure I would have difficulties painting His face. It has often been said that a man's face is the window of his soul. Sorrow never begets laughter, and intense mirth is never accompanied by sobs. How can any painter harmonize pity, pain, and pleasure in one picture? If I were an artist, I would have to paint four pictures of the Lord, but they would hang together in one special gallery.

The shining face (Matt. 17:2)

The first painting would be based on what happened on the Mount of Transfiguration, where the Lord's face shone as the sun. The shining face seems to be characteristic of all who live in the immediate presence of God. Evidence of this may be found in the experiences of Moses and Daniel, and elsewhere in the Scriptures. We are told that, at the resurrection of Christ, two angels appeared in white and testified that Christ had risen from the dead. *Phillip's* translation says, "Their faces were dazzling." *The New English Bible* says: "they shone." Yet, these incidents are different from what we are privileged to see on the Mount of Transfiguration. With men and angels, the glory resembled a holy sunburn; it was something that came from without, stamping its mark on those present. With Christ, the radiance came from within. The glory that Christ had known from the beginning, the majesty of His inner self, broke through the frail barrier of human flesh, and the heavenly sunshine shone out for all to see. The question concerning His true identity was answered on the mountain. But what artist could effectively paint that scene?

The suffering face (Isa. 52:14)

This remarkable verse predicted that "his visage was so marred more than any man." This has been translated as being so marred as to be unrecognizable. That the Lord's face should be twisted by agony and bruised by punches makes all wise men shudder. Christ had been mercilessly scourged until the flesh on His back was lacerated and broken; He had been forced to carry His cross until even the soldiers recognized He could carry it no more. He had been nailed to that cross, which in turn had been lifted and dropped into the prepared hole in the ground. Then the entire weight of Christ's body had cruelly sagged on the nails. He had suffered anguish beyond measure, and as a result His face had become distorted by pain. It seemed a very long way from the shining face to the suffering face, and we should remember the distance was only bridged by His redeeming love for men and women.

The solemn face (Rev. 6:15-17)

"And every bondman, and every free man, hid themselves in the dens and in the rocks of the mountains; And said to the mountains and rocks, Fall on us, and hide us from the face of him that sitteth on the throne, and from the wrath of the Lamb: For the great day of his wrath is come; and who shall be able to stand?" "It is appointed unto men once to die, but after this, the judgment" (Heb. 9:27). For many people, this subject has become the forgotten or ignored part of Bible teaching. Knowledge begets responsibility, and all who have heard the gospel must account to God and His Son for the reception given to that message. The Lord died to make forgiveness possible; but, if people ignore or reject what God has done and said, there remains "a certain fearful looking for of judgment.... He that despised Moses' law died without mercy under two or three witnesses: Of how much sorer punishment, suppose ye, shall he be thought worthy, who hath trodden under foot the Son of God, and hath counted the blood of the covenant, wherewith he was sanctified, an unholy thing, and hath done despite unto the Spirit of Grace?" (Heb. 10:27-29).

The serene face (Rev. 22:4)

The fourth in the collection of paintings would be based on the aforementioned text. "And they shall see his face; and his name shall be in their foreheads." Probably there will be many thrilling and wonderful sights in heaven, but there is reason to believe the face of Jesus will outshine them all. The closing chapters of the Bible describe many beautiful things. The redeemed saints will see the river of the water of life, the New Jerusalem, and all the marvelous things provided by God in a realm where sickness, pain, and limitations of every kind will be unknown. There will be a choir in which will sing "ten thousand times ten thousand, and thousands of thousands." There will be no hospitals, no cemeteries, no funeral parlors, no hovels, no dirt, and nothing to displease. But, amidst the galaxies of shining stars, none will shine more brightly than the face of Him who made all this possible for redeemed sinners. "And they shall see his face." Blessed is the man and happy is the woman able to say with assurance:

And I shall see Him face to face,
And tell the story — saved by grace.

THE SAVIOR . . . and the missing lamb

(MATTHEW 26:19)

To appreciate and understand the significance of the Lord's final Passover, it is necessary to be aware of the changes that had taken place in Israel. When Moses first issued the instructions regarding the feast, the observance was relatively easy. There was only one consecrated meeting place in the land; it was the tabernacle where the lamb was slain. Doubtless, each household shared in the ceremony. Later, when Palestine became the national home of the Jews, a temple was erected; and there, as in the tabernacle, the sacrifice was offered. As the centuries passed, vast changes came to the nation.

The different circumstances

When our Lord ministered upon earth, the Passover had become the greatest of all feasts, and the crowds attending it so vast, that even laws had to be changed to accommodate the new features. Whereas formerly all people were obliged to worship on the consecrated grounds of the sanctuary, the new circumstances made it necessary for "the holy ground" to be extended as far as Bethany. People were permitted to pitch their tents anywhere they could find room. *Josephus* describes how a certain governor named Cestius asked the high priest to ascertain the number of lambs slain at the annual festival. He wished to inform Nero in order to make the emperor understand the importance of the Jewish nation. The number came to 256,500. *Josephus* further relates that one lamb represented between ten (the minimum) and twenty people who participated in sharing the sacrifice. Therefore, the number of worshipers at the Passover feast would have been approximately three million.

The definite conclusion

Jerusalem was one of the greatest cities in the world, and its temple was recognized as one of the most beautiful sights men could behold. The arrival of millions of visitors created problems of many kinds. At the Passover feast it became necessary to supply a quarter of a million lambs, and latecomers probably had great difficulty in purchasing their offering. The idea that Jesus was crucified on a Friday is questionable. Had that been the case, He could not have remained in the grave for three days and nights prior to His resurrection on the first day of the week. The Lord was crucified on Wednesday, and it is now known that this was the day when the lambs were slain in the temple. Realizing the need for adequate preparation, the disciples reminded the Lord of the approaching feast and asked if they could go ahead to Jerusalem to do what needed to be done.

The detailed consideration

There were strict laws that governed preparation for the Passover. Every house had to be completely spring-cleaned so that no particle of leaven remained. Even rafters had to be dusted. A suitable meeting place had to be found and furnished. Bread, wine, and bitter herbs had to be purchased, but greatest in importance was the securing of a lamb to be sacrificed. This had to be taken to the temple and certified by the priest that it was without blemish. Various other details also demanded attention. Peter and John were commissioned to attend to these requirements. We now know that Jesus had made prior arrangements with an unknown friend, and the possibility exists that many of these necessities had been arranged prior to the arrival of the disciples.

The delightful claim

When all was in readiness, the Lord, having reached the city, sat down with His friends to celebrate the feast. Those men were surely puzzled. Normally, at a certain point in the proceedings, every participant took a piece of the roasted lamb and ate it, even as Moses had commanded. The disciples saw the bread, the wine, and the bitter herbs, but there was no lamb. How could any person celebrate Passover without a lamb? It was then that Jesus seemed to say, "You are asking, 'Where is the lamb?' We do not need one for I AM THE LAMB! This is my flesh; eat, believe and live." He had said, "With desire, I have desired to eat this Passover with you before I suffer" (Luke 22:15). We may never understand the intensity of the Lord's wishes. He was about to teach the disciples that they would never again need a lamb nor even attend a Passover feast. He was instituting a new law and a new feast which superceded the old ordinances. The Passover expressed the past; the communion service embraced the future. Even the regular day of observance was being replaced by "as oft as ye will, do this in remembrance of me." What happened to the lamb provided by Peter and John? Was it used by the owner of the house? Did it stand unwanted in a corner of the yard? There is no record of any New Testament Christian ever attending another Passover Feast, unless it was to preach the gospel to the crowds gathered on that occasion. Truly, old things had passed away; all things had become new. Jesus was all they needed.

THE TRUE CHRISTIAN . . . and how he may be recognized

I shall always remember the young woman in Wales who asked if I would answer a question. She prefaced her remarks with the statement that students in the University at Cardiff had been debating it every lunch hour for three weeks, and no answer had been forthcoming. "Sir", she said, "What is a Christian?" Her expression suggested she sought an argument and not information. During the moments that followed, Paul seemed to supply me with what was needed. He had described four word pictures in the Epistle to the Ephesians which related to her problem.

A student . . . decision (Mark 1:16-20)

Paul in Ephesians 5:1 said, "Be ye therefore followers of God, as dear children." The word suggested a student following a teacher walking along a country road. Originally there were few schools as we know them, philosophers strolled in the fields and streets, and all who wished to learn walked behind, gleaning words of wisdom as they fell from the teacher's lips. The Savior had adopted the same method; He walked the dusty highways of Palestine, teaching as He went. The Greek word for disciples was *matheetees*, which meant a "learner; a follower; a disciple." When the earliest followers of Christ left their occupations to become itinerant preachers, they indicated: (1) They believed Jesus had knowledge they needed to acquire. (2) They were anxious to stay near to Him so that whatever He said they would hear and hopefully remember. The same truths are evident with all who profess to become Christians.

A slave . . . devotion (Exod. 21:5-6)

"Be ye therefore followers of God, as dear children; And walk in love . . . Not with eyeservice, as menpleasers; but as the [*slaves*] of Christ" (Eph. 5:1; 6:6). The word translated "slaves" is *doulos*, which means "a bondslave." A bondslave was one who preferred to remain in the service of his master than to be liberated as a freeman. When the year of liberation arrived, all slaves were automatically released; but, when a slave preferred to remain, he was required to stand at the door of his house where the master would pierce his ear as a sign that, of his own volition, he had requested to stay. During years of service, the slave obviously came to respect and love his master. Necessity made him a slave, but love made him a bondslave. This is probably the most obvious evidence in the growth of a Christian. He loves the Lord to such a degree that nothing in existence could compensate for his loss of joy should their fellowship cease.

A soldier . . . discipline (Eph. 6:10-18)

"Finally, my brethren. . . . Put on the whole armour of God, that ye may be able to stand against the wiles of the devil." One of the Bible's greatest illustrations of this truth is found in Genesis 14:14. When Lot was taken captive by heathen kings, Abraham took 318 bondslaves and went to rescue his nephew. It may be safely assumed that he had no fear of betrayal from his soldiers; they were trained in his own house — they were bondslaves. Paul spoke about another great battle, the conflict against the powers of darkness, and urged his readers to put on the whole armor of God. Taking his illustration from the uniform and weapons of Roman soldiers, he proceeded to mention protection for every part of the body — *except the back*! Caesar probably believed that if his soldiers ever ran from danger, they deserved to die! Each man had a covering for his loins, his chest, his feet, and his head. A sword was to be in his hand, and, thus prepared, either the Roman or the Christian was ready for battle. The followers of Christ were never promised an easy road to heaven. Life was a battlefield, and the Lord depended upon trusted bondslaves to win conflicts against evil.

A statesman . . . dignity (Eph. 6:20)

Paul asked the Ephesians to pray earnestly for him, saying, *"I am an ambassador in bonds*" Statesmen are never chosen from among the inhabitants of skid row. More often than not, the finest graduates of the university are chosen for such high honors. They are to become the representatives of their country in a foreign land. An ambassador remembers he represents his homeland and acts accordingly. Paul was conscious of the fact that his citizenship was in heaven. His attitude, conduct, and speech always testified of that fact. He was God's representative in an alien world, and even his enemies should be able to see the evidence of his high calling. Paul was a man apart! He was certainly a true Christian, and all who would covet his success should emulate his example by becoming (1) A student of Christ. (2) A bondslave of Christ. (3) A soldier willing to live and die for his cause. (4) A man who walks worthy of his high calling. These are the hallmarks of a true Christian.

ANNA . . . and her cure for loneliness

(LUKE 2:36-37)

This lady who lived in the temple was a remarkable woman. It is claimed the earliest age at which marriage was permitted was twelve years. If she were married at that age, she became a widow at the age of twenty-one and thereafter remained unmarried for eighty-four years. If this computation be correct, she was 105 years of age when she saw the infant Christ. It was significant that, after the death of her husband, she never remarried. It has been claimed her name meant "gracious;" and, if this was indicative of her character, this charming young woman was a most desirable person. That she remained a widow suggests possibilities.

Her true virtue

When her husband died, her home and future appeared to be in jeopardy; and Anna went to live either in, or very close to, the sanctuary. Others in her situation might have become extremely critical of the ways of God, but this young widow sought the Lord's presence instead of criticizing Him. It is written she "departed not from the temple, but served God with fastings and prayers night and day." Bereavement would temporarily devastate her soul; but, when sorrow began to wane, she did not waste time asking unanswerable questions why God had permitted her personal tragedy. She prayed and came to the most important decision of her life. Aware of loneliness within her soul, Anna sought refuge in the sanctuary. Whenever she felt her burdens were too heavy to be carried, she placed her hand into the hand of God and left it there. Her constant presence in the sanctuary became known to the visitors, and finally Anna was considered to be a prophetess. Probably she was not a preacher or one who foretold the future but rather a counselor, a guide for other women who came with their problems to the Lord. Anna was a true mother in Israel, and we may never know how many young women were helped by the gracious words of this admirable lady. Doubtless she felt the presence of God at all times; it was extremely difficult to feel lonely when she enjoyed such excellent company.

Her tremendous value

It has been said she "served God with fastings and prayers night and day" (Luke 2:37). David, many years earlier, had exclaimed, "As the hart panteth after the water brooks, so panteth my soul after thee, O God. My soul thirsteth for God, for the living God" (Ps. 42:1-2). It would appear the mantle of David had fallen upon this woman of a later age. She hungered for fellowship with God, and nothing else could satisfy the inherent longings of her soul. This was, and ever will remain, the introduction to worship. Anna had eyes only for God, and that possibly explained why she never sought another husband. God was aware of her dedicated service; such souls were hard to find in a very attractive world. We might ask the reason for her constant dedication. Even the need for food could not entice her from the altar. She had a burden upon her soul; she meant business! It is impossible to hide the Savior from such a seeking heart. Happy indeed are those people whose steps are ordered by the Lord; who enter the sanctuary to see HIM.

Her thrilling vision

It was a wonderful moment when the aged lady met the mother of Jesus. Already Simeon had surprised a crowd of onlookers by his excitement and utterances; but, when the prophetess came to add her testimony, the angels surely smiled. She "spake of him to all that looked for redemption in Jerusalem." When she looked into the face of the infant Christ, she announced to bystanders that the Messiah had arrived! How did she learn so much in such a short time? The same question might have been asked of John the Baptist, who recognized the Lamb of God who would remove the sin of the world. When God was about to destroy Sodom, He asked a question, saying, "Shall I hide from Abraham that thing which I do?" (Gen. 18:17). It is impossible to be close to God and remain unaware of His intentions. To share God's fellowship is to share His confidence. Divine revelation is not always governed by academic standards. There are occasions when a day at Christ's feet is more instructive than a complete course in a college, but blessed and privileged are they who enjoy both.

Anna was too busy to be lonely. (1) She saw. (2) She listened. (3) She knew. Her ministry might be summarized under four headings. She worshiped; she interceded; she fasted; she served. We may not know how she found time for all four, but obviously she did! She was one of the busiest and most attractive ladies in Israel. Wise indeed are they who learn from her memorable example. When calamity overwhelms the soul, it is wise to remember that God is too wise to make mistakes and too loving to be unkind. If He permits unwelcome difficulties to harass His children, it is better to share our problems with Him than it is to run away. Anna probably knew that even the darkest and longest nights were followed by a sunrise!

THE LORD JESUS . . . who ruined a service

(LUKE 4:28-29)

It was the Sabbath day in Nazareth, and respectable citizens were in the synagogue. They wondered if there would be any visitors, for it was the custom that strangers would read the Scripture chosen for that particular day. Suddenly, a wave of interest passed through the audience. Jesus, whom they knew, had just entered, and the rabbi was about to give to Him the sacred scroll. They had heard much about the Carpenter, for recently, so it was claimed, He had healed people in other synagogues. Could it be possible He might repeat His performance in their midst? They watched and listened carefully; the service could become exciting!

The unique choice . . . "he found the place!"

Certain passages from the law were always selected, but with apparent deliberation Jesus unrolled the scroll until He found what He desired and then began to read: "The Spirit of the Lord is upon me . . . To preach the acceptable year of the Lord" (Luke 4:18-19; Isa. 61:1-2). Almost every day the Lord referred to the ancient writings and endorsed what had been written. He knew what He desired to say, and found the scripture upon which to base His message. When He cited the statements made by Isaiah and indicated He had been anointed to preach the gospel to the poor, He made a claim that later turned the congregation into a mob. Wise is the preacher who expounds the Word of God and bases every claim on the infallable message of the prophets. It is a tragedy when orators speak for lengthy periods and say nothing!

The unexpected climax . . . "And he closed the book."

It is interesting to note that Jesus finished at a strange place. He was reading from the writings of Isaiah but omitted to mention an important statement. "To proclaim the acceptable year of the LORD, *and the day of vengeance of our God* . . . " Although He proceeded to mention other statements of Isaiah, that one omission suggests deliberation. Christ had come to earth *not* to execute judgment, *not* to exact vengeance upon the guilty, but to *open a highway* to the heart of God. His arrival was meant to introduce an age of grace, and all who recognized that fact found new happiness in a closer relationship with the Almighty.

The unsurpassed claim . . . "This day is this scripture fulfilled."

It should always be remembered the writings quoted by Jesus were only a small part of the prophet's statements. All Jews believed Isaiah referred to the Messiah and, with the exception of chapter 53, still acknowledge the book to be messianic. When their Carpenter-Citizen said, "This day is this scripture fulfilled in your ears," He began to tread on dangerous ground. They acknowledged that He spoke graciously, but He was only the son of Joseph! Had success gone to His head? Was He beginning to make outrageous claims because He had grown too big for His sandals? Thus did Jesus begin to advance His claims, and as then, so now. Either He was what He claimed, or He was a charlatan.

The unforgettable charm . . . "the gracious words which proceeded out of his mouth."

Jesus was an enthralling speaker; His language was choice and beautiful; His manner was gracious and charming; His face radiated confidence and happiness. Children would never have climbed upon His knees to be cuddled if He were miserable, irritable, and forbidding. He said He had come from God, and His manner endorsed the claim. All who represent heaven should emulate His example.

The unusual challenge . . . "But I tell you . . . truth."

It should always be remembered that the Lord did not begin to preach words of condemnation until the listeners exhibited unbelief. They thought Him to be just the son of the village carpenter; He was an upstart; and, should He desire approbation, He should perform some of the healing tricks that had made Him famous. Momentarily, they forgot they were supposed to be worshiping in a synagogue. They wanted to turn the sanctuary into a circus, to replace exposition with entertainment. The cutting edge of His sermon began to pierce their consciences. He reminded them that God's blessing had gone to outsiders such as the woman of Sarepta and Naaman the leper, people far removed from the temple and Israel. He was trying to tell them He had come unto His own, who were unwilling to receive Him. The convicting power of the Holy Spirit will either make a man furious or penitent.

The undisturbed confidence . . . "But he passing through the midst of them went his way."

"And all they in the synagogue, when they heard these things, were filled with wrath, And rose up, and thrust him out of the city, and led him unto the brow of the hill whereon their city was built, that they might cast him down headlong. But he passing through the midst of them went his way." The people who tried to murder Jesus were incensed. As hatred dominated their thinking, they pushed Him toward the precipice. Yet, His serenity remained undisturbed. He was safe and He knew it. Until the hour of His crucifixion arrived, no power could hurt Him. He knew, as we should know, it pays to have God as a Father and friend!

JESUS . . . and the untouchables

(LUKE 17:11-19)

Somewhere near a dusty highway in Samaria or Galilee was a leper colony in which strange things had taken place. A Samaritan was living with Jews! What had been impossible when the men were healthy suddenly became a reality in sickness. Racial barriers had disappeared; for, with the approach of death, the lepers had been forced to consider more important matters. Then one day the news reached the colony that the great Healer from Nazareth would soon be passing along the highway, and their animated discussions reflected the hope within their souls.

A story of fear

It is almost impossible for people in the western world to understand what it meant to be a leper. Today the terrible disease has almost been banished from civilization, but unfortunately there are parts of the world where the scourge still appears, where lepers are immediately segregated from other people, and little is heard of them again. Relatives are compelled to make a difficult choice, either to accompany loved ones into permanent isolation or to remain separated forever. Alas, in India and other eastern countries, leprosy is still a dreaded disease, and it is still possible to witness scenes reminiscent of Bible times. During the years when Jesus was upon the earth, there was little, if any, hope for the cleansing of lepers; medical science had nothing to offer stricken people. Once a person became infected, the only unanswered question was: "How long have I to live?"

A story of faith

When the news of Christ's approach reached the camp, seething excitement gripped the inmates, for they had heard amazing stories of His ability to cleanse lepers. It can only be imagined what discussions took place, for the Mosaic law was very explicit in regulations governing the conduct of lepers. Any infected person who threatened the health of other people was put to death by stoning. Lepers not only had to give adequate warning if they had to cross a road; they were commanded to stay as far away as possible from citizens in every town or village. Therefore it would have been an unforgivable offense if they approached Jesus directly. Any request would need to be shouted from a distance. Probably the men deliberated for a long time whether or not to solicit His aid. However formidable the risk, it would have been suicidal to remain in their camp. Once they reached that decision, subsequent actions were not quite as difficult.

"And as he entered into a certain village, there met him ten men that were lepers, which stood afar off: And they lifted up their voices, and said, Jesus, Master, have mercy on us. And when he saw them, he said unto them, Go show yourselves unto the priests. And it came to pass, that, as they went, they were cleansed" (Luke 17:12-14). The Lord's command presented a new problem. Only *cleansed* lepers went to the priests. How could they obey Jesus without running the risk of being punished for their action? Had they remained motionless, they would never have been cleansed. To hear the command of Christ is one thing, but to believe is another. Nevertheless, to obey the Lord is better than the first two together. Hearing the gospel never saved anybody, but faith expressed in obedience to the command of the Savior can accomplish the impossible. "As they *went* they were *cleansed.*"

A story of fervor

When the healing and cleansing power of Christ reached those stricken men, unprecedented excitement flooded their souls, and soon nine men filled with happiness rushed toward the home of the priests. The other man, the Samaritan, remained motionless as though he had been turned to stone. He wondered if he were dreaming; he was clean! What should he do? Should he follow his companions to the abode of the authorities? No, that could wait; he would like to thank his kindly Benefactor. Thoughtfully he went in search of Jesus, who asked, "Where are the nine? There are not found that returned to give glory to God, save this stranger. And he said unto him . . . thy faith hath made thee whole." Is there a suggestion here that the Samaritan received an additional blessing? To be delivered was something of incalculable worth, but to be made whole might have been greater. It would appear that the limbs damaged by the disease suddenly regained their original shape. No man ever suffered because gratitude brought him to the feet of Jesus. Today, Christians sing "Thank You, Lord, for saving my soul; Thank You, Lord, for making me whole." The leper, had he known the chorus, would have sung its message fervently; he had been made *whole*

Are we so far removed from the ancient scene? The disease of sin is far more dangerous than leprosy. One destroys the body; the other destroys both body and soul. (See Matt. 10:28.) Mingled fear and faith may bring us to Christ, but only gratitude keeps us there. Everybody seems anxious to seek Christ's aid, but few remember to thank Him. Are we among the nine?

JESUS . . . and the man from another convention

(LUKE 9:49-50)

The special meeting . . . it was unauthorized!

The disciples had been commissioned to preach the gospel, and had walked the highways of Palestine seeking congregations. Probably it was during this time they encountered the "alien" preacher. Seeing a crowd ahead, John and his companion were attracted to the gathering. People were praising God and were evidently enthralled. A strange man was preaching about Jesus and was actually releasing demoniacs from Satan's power. John was amazed and impetuously went forward to ask by whose authority the man acted as he did. If people wished to be healed, they should go to the proper source. John rebuked the preacher, telling him not to interfere in things that were not his concern.

The strange messenger . . . he was not a regular disciple!

He was unknown; he belonged to another convention! Poor John! He had cataracts upon his eyes and was willing for people to remain enslaved rather than admit the possibility that God could use a stranger to do His will. Perhaps the most important lesson any man can learn is that he is not the only pebble on God's beach! There are those who sincerely believe they have a franchise on God's activities; to be associated with any movement other than their own is suspect. Anyone anxious to serve Christ should join the "authorized" convention, receive his papers, and go to work for Jesus. This is not only unscriptural, it is absurd!

The stupid men . . . they might have prevented a revival!

It is impossible to know how long the preacher had been operating, nor can we know what might have taken place if John had not interfered. Souls were being blessed, devils expelled, and the Savior glorified. Maybe the man told John to "mind his own business" and thereafter continued his work. On the other hand, he might have refrained from further service. Whatever John's motives, he was completely unjustified in trying to prevent something that God was blessing. If the man had been magnifying his own personal greatness or using his gift to bring financial gain, then John would have been within his rights.

But the unknown preacher was glorifying the Son of God, and it was arrogant bigotry that interfered in his activities. Unfortunately, our world is filled with monopolies. Unless a man belongs to a trade union, he is prevented from working in certain industries; unless a man belongs to an authorized convention, his religious activities are curtailed, and many doors of opportunity close before him. When a person begins to testify for Christ, the question is soon asked, "To what church do you belong?" If an unwelcome answer is received, many listeners refrain from further contact.

A man should be judged by his accomplishments, by the quality of his message, by his identification with Christ. It is thought-provoking to see and hear pastors criticizing a successful brother when their own church is empty. Within the body of Christ there should be no man-made barriers to ruin fellowship. Any man who exalts the cross of Christ is worthy of support.

The sublime master . . . and His delightful command!

"And Jesus said unto him, Forbid him not: for he that is not against us is for us." The Lord was very patient and wonderful. He did not scold His unwise disciple but gently led him into paths of wisdom. Harsh words and scathing condemnation were never present in the life of the Savior, unless He was being confronted by the sinister plots of His antagonists. It is worthy of attention that, soon afterward, Jesus again found it necessary to repeat the lesson already taught. "And it came to pass, when the time was come that he should be received up, he steadfastly set his face to go to Jerusalem, And sent messengers . . . into a village of the Samaritans. . . . And they did not receive him. . . . And when his disciples James and John saw this, they said, Lord, wilt thou that we command fire to come down from heaven, and consume them, even as Elias did?" (Luke 9: 51-54). Poor John, he had so much to learn. For a time he appeared to be at war with everybody. He rebuked the unknown preacher and was willing to cremate a village of unfriendly Samaritans. When Jesus said, "Ye know not what manner of spirit ye are of. For the Son of man is not come to destroy men's lives, but to save them," the disciple was given another opportunity to look into the heart of God.

It should always be remembered that love is the cement that unites living stones in the walls of Christ's church. Enmity, bitterness, and strife are the bulldozers which destroy, in moments, what took years to erect. It is better to love than to hate; it is more beneficial to help than hurt. If along the highways of life strange workers for Christ are encountered, it is better not to ask their church affiliations but rather seek to know if they truly love the Lord and His sacred Word. Dogmatic people often agree on 99% of doctrine but prefer to argue over an insignificant detail. Charles Haddon Spurgeon, the famous British preacher, used to say: "There will be three wonders in heaven. The first, we shall see people there we never expected to find. The second, many will be absent we did expect to find. The third, the greatest wonder of all, we shall be there!" The sure way to avoid criticism of others is to look steadily into the face of Jesus.

BARABBAS . . . the most fortunate man in the world

(LUKE 23:25)

Dear Barabbas,

We have always desired to speak with you, because what we know of your history intrigues us. Unfortunately, you are now beyond our reach; but, if it were possible, we would ask a few questions.

Your God

We have been told that your name suggests you were the son of a rabbi. Whether or not that was the case we cannot be sure; but, to say the least, the suggestion leads to strange possibilities. When you were young, did you ever attend a synagogue? Did you ever study in your father's school — that is, if he was a rabbi? It is very difficult for us to comprehend what appear to be extremes in your experiences. We are sure you knew about the faith of your fathers. How then did you become an insurrectionist and a murderer? Is it possible that you shared the common conviction that the Romans were enemies? Did your father's ideas appear to be obnoxious because they promoted tolerance whereas you desired action — fast? Is it possible that you considered opposition to the enemy as service acceptable in the sight of God? Did you believe you were God's instrument to expel those heathens from the Holy Land?

Your guilt

A medical doctor named Luke wrote about you and said that "for a certain sedition made in the city, and for murder, [you were] cast into prison" (Luke 23:19). Barabbas, that was a terrible thing to do! Were you overtaken in a raid? Was your life in danger as the soldiers surrounded you? Desperately, did you try to defend yourself or escape, and in the struggle did you drive your dagger through a man's heart? We wish you were here to tell us about these unknown details. Of course, we understand how merciless the Romans were, and once you were incarcerated in that dungeon you had no hope of escape. Did you have a decent trial, and did the judge at least understand your point of view? Well, it does not really matter, for your case was, as we say, cut and dried; they were determined to make an example of their notorious prisoner.

Your grief

Barabbas, we are really in doubt at this point; we have no information whatsoever. The Bible portrays you as a fearless, unrelenting criminal, and that might really have been true, but did you ever feel remorse although you never said so? If your father was a religious leader, did you become concerned because you had broken his heart? In your quieter moments, did you ever worry, just a little, because you might have broken God's heart? If so, we can understand. Sometimes, our pride is so strong that our deeper feelings are suppressed. We resent people who probe into our secrets. Were you like that? Did you shrug your shoulders and condemn those feelings as weaknesses of the flesh? When the news came that you were to be liberated because a mob had chosen you instead of a Carpenter from Nazareth, were you surprised? Of course, you knew all about Jesus of Nazareth; He had preached and healed your countrymen when you were an insurrectionist. Did you ever wonder if He had appeared to champion your cause?

Your gratitude

When they opened your prison door and removed the chains from your wrists and feet, did you wonder if you were having a dream? Oh, maybe some of your fellow brigands had been in the crowd, but the choice had been so widespread that you knew instinctively there had to be some other reason why the stupid people chose you in order to crucify Israel's best Friend. When the wonderment had ceased, did you make your way to Golgotha to see for yourself the Man who had died on your cross? Well, Barabbas, as a matter of fact, there is a legend that said you did, but people of a later age do not know whether to trust legends or not. That is the reason why we would love to be able to speak face to face with you.

If you went to Calvary, if you stood beneath His cross and looked into His bloodstained face, what did you think at that moment? Things could have been so different; you could have been nailed on that tree. It seems strange to us that your name was never mentioned again by those who wrote our Bible. You disappeared from public life, and that seems to infer that you never returned to the notoriety of former years. Oh, Barabbas, there are many questions we would like to ask you. You see, we think we can share your feelings — at least to a point. Perhaps you would appreciate the words of one of our songs:

Lord, help me never to forget
The old, old rugged cross:
Let all its scenes before me lie
Until all else seems dross.
Oh, help me then to understand
How great was Thy rich grace;
I should have died upon that cross
But *Thou didst take my place.*

BIBLE MEN . . . and their great opportunities

It has been said that "Opportunity knocks once at the door of the human heart. What is done then might decide destiny." The following studies endorse that claim.

A lost man . . . dying

Calvary's hill had become strangely quiet! The crowd that had demanded Christ's death now seemed fascinated as they watched their victim. Even the soldiers were staring hard at the One whose hands they had nailed to the cross. One of the criminals crucified with Jesus had electrified the crowd with a strange request. He had asked for admittance to Paradise; and Jesus, acknowledging the request, had given peace to the suppliant. It was all so strange. How could He possibly do such a thing? Was He not another common criminal? But there was another man whose raucous voice disturbed the silence. He was swearing at everybody. Why did he not keep his mouth shut? He was disturbing everyone; he was a nuisance. A soldier should quiet the fellow! There was no need; death was about to silence him forever. What a shame! His companion had found eternal peace, and that same peace might have filled the soul of the second thief. Alas, he might have become famous, but he lost his opportunity. He was at the very door of heaven, but his stupidity, not the nails, prevented his entrance. (See Luke 23:39.)

A learned man . . . delaying

The Supreme Court was hushed! An outstanding Doctor of the Law was about to address the assembly. Those pesky Jewish preachers should be taken to the waiting room; why should their presence defile the chamber? The Honorable Member will now speak. "Then stood there up one in the council, a Pharisee, named Gamaliel, a doctor of the law, had in reputation among all the people, and commanded to put the apostles forth a little space." The man was a genius; his knowledge of historical events was vast and unassailable. The audience listened carefully as he proceeded to explain his philosophy. What a speaker! What a man! He was nearing conclusion. "And now I say unto you, Refrain from these men, and let them alone: for if this counsel or this work be of men, it will come to nought: But if it be of God, ye cannot overthrow it; lest haply ye be found even to fight against God." Gentlemen, be wise, do nothing. Just wait and see. And, apparently, that is exactly what Gamaliel did for the rest of his life. When the power of the risen Christ turned the world upside down, he remained in the background. He watched the game; he even appreciated some of the players. But he never became a participant; he was too scared of getting hurt. (See Acts 5:34-42.)

A little man . . . deciding

The street was crowded with excited people, and the little businessman could not conceal his curiosity. What in the wide world was happening? Zaccheus went out of his office to meet the most wonderful Man he had ever seen. "And he sought to see Jesus *who he was*!" We cannot help but ask where Zaccheus had been during the amazing three years of Christ's ministry. Surely all people knew *who Jesus was*! No, the tax-gatherer, so hated by the citizens because he worked for the accursed Romans, had reciprocated; he hated them also. He only saw people; and, because he was so short, they probably appeared to be very tall — and very big hypocrites. But the excitement in the street was irresistible. Something was happening, and suddenly he ceased looking at Jews. He was sick of them anyway. Thank God for making trees; they were perfect grandstands from which to see the show! "And Jesus . . . saw him. . . . And [Zaccheus] made haste, and came down, and received him joyfully." And that night they had dinner together. Simon's mother-in-law would have loved the little tax-gatherer. He seized his opportunity. (See Luke 19:1-10.)

A liberated man . . . declaring

The former demoniac was climbing the hill; he was intensely grateful, very puzzled, and a little apprehensive. He paused to look back, and his face reflected a keen disappointment. His Friend, Jesus of Nazareth, was in that little fishing boat going farther and farther away. Those stupid people and their swine! They had asked Him to go away, and He had gone. "Why could I not also be in that boat?" No, he had a job to do. Jesus had asked him to testify in the village and he would do it if it killed him! "And he went his way, and published throughout the whole city how great things Jesus had done unto him." (See Luke 8:37-39.) If that man had ever met Saul of Tarsus, they would have talked for hours! Real opportunities for service may seem rare, and yet they are all around us — they are everywhere. (Reprinted in part from the author's commentary, *Mark's Superb Gospel*; pp. 44-46.)

JOHN . . . who believed in believing

The apostle John had a favorite term that he used constantly throughout his writings. The word *believe* may be found ninety times in his Gospel, and John explained that this was the reason why he wrote his book. He said: "And many other signs truly did Jesus . . . But these are written, that ye might believe that Jesus is the Christ, the Son of God; and that believing ye might have life through his name" (John 20:30-31). This was probably the result of the apostle's fellowship with the Savior, for Jesus also emphasized the importance of believing. We now choose four of the incidents mentioned by the beloved disciple.

Constantly satisfied (John 6:35)

"*He that believeth on me shall never thirst.*" It becomes clear that Jesus was not referring to any intellectual apprehension of theological doctrine. He was thinking of the enthusiasm that takes a believer toward a desired goal. This is not a picture of an athlete sitting comfortably amidst the luxury of a stadium dressing room. It is the thrilling picture of a man straining every nerve in a supreme effort to win a race. When a believer approaches the Lord with that kind of passion, it becomes clear all he desires is the approbation of his Master. Jesus indicated that such seekers would never thirst because a well of living water would become active within their souls. (See John 4:14.)

Conspicuously successful (John 7:38)

"He that believeth on me . . . out of his belly [or inmost being] shall flow rivers of living water." This promise was given by the Lord during the final day of the great feast at Jerusalem. The supplies of water in the city had been depleted, and visitors had reason to complain of their tormenting conditions. They had become intensely thirsty and could only think of their need to drink. They did not understand why Jesus delivered His invitation. He thought of a dying world where the living water of the gospel was urgently needed. He realized He would soon return to heaven, and the work of international evangelism would become the responsibility of fishermen from Galilee. Long afterward, John remembered the Master's words and explained: "But this spake he of the Spirit, which they that believe on him should receive: for the Holy Ghost was not yet given, because that Jesus was not yet glorified" (John 7:39). A personal coronation of the Savior is always a prerequisite of the outpouring of the Holy Spirit.

Completely safe (John 11:26)

"And whosoever liveth and believeth in me shall never die." The streets of Bethany were probably crowded when Martha, the sister of the deceased Lazarus, went to meet the Lord. The news of the impending arrival of Jesus probably brought people from all directions, and the nearby cemetery was a grim reminder that, sooner or later, every citizen would be laid to rest in that place. Jesus was aware of this undeniable fact, and yet He said that whosoever believed in Him would never die. The Lord gave a new meaning to the death of saints, and that was the reason why Luke, referring to the death of Stephen, said, "He fell asleep." (See Acts 7:60.) When the first martyr of the church awakened in heaven, he discovered the scenery had changed, but his Lord was the same as ever. This thrilling truth enabled Paul to write: "Death is swallowed up in victory. O death, where is thy sting? O grave, where is thy victory?" (1 Cor. 15:54-55).

Conspicuously superior (John 14:12)

"He that believeth on me, the works that I do shall he do also; and greater works than these shall he do; because I go unto my Father." It is extremely difficult to read these words without realizing that something has gone wrong — with us! The Lord predicted that our ministry would surpass His — *if we believed.* It is true the ministry of the church now reaches the whole world, whereas Jesus never traveled more than 150 miles from His birthplace. It is also true that, whereas Jesus opened the eyes of a few blind men, the church through medical science has opened the eyes of millions of men and women. Nevertheless, is that the final interpretation of the promise of Christ? It must be admitted that in certain areas of activity, the apathy of the church is disappointing. We appear to be working hard and accomplishing little. *Could it be that we have not truly believed?* Adequate organization is a necessity; wise planning is to be desired at all times. But, according to the writings of John, the power to drive our machinery is only supplied by faith in the risen Christ. Without it, our efforts can only be second rate.

CHRIST . . . and His once-only visits

One of the intriguing features associated with the Lord's ministry was that He only visited certain places once. He went several times to Bethany and Jerusalem, and His itineraries in Galilee often covered the same ground. Nevertheless, for some inscrutable reason, He only went once to certain villages, but each time this happened, something spectacular took place. We are therefore convinced His actions were deliberately planned.

To reveal a mission (John 4:5)

"Then cometh he to a city of Samaria, which is called Sychar." The Lord probably went to that part of the country often, but there is no record that He ever visited the well at Sychar except to encounter a very degraded woman, who was obliged to draw water when other people were absent. To travel during the heat of midday was unthinkable; dogs knew better than to run around at that time of the day. Yet it is written: "And he *must* needs go through Samaria" (v. 4). It would have been impossible to meet that woman at any other time, unless a visit were made to her house! To do that would have been unwise, for she lived in a place of ill repute. The story of what happened at the well is known universally; there is no need to repeat its details. Early in the Lord's ministry He made it clear that the love of God could not be confined by man-made restrictions. This woman was a Samaritan; she lived among other Samaritans; and, in spite of the denunciations made by the priests, these untouchables were precious in God's sight. This was the purpose of Jesus' mission to earth — to break down the middle wall of partition and to unite all people by His redeeming love. This was revealed for the first time at Sychar's well.

To relieve a mother (Luke 7:11)

"And it came to pass the day after, that he went into a city called Nain." There is no mention that He ever went to this place on any other occasion. His arrival was planned to coincide with a funeral coming through the gateway. Had He arrived earlier or later, He would have missed that procession. This was the second time the bereaved mother had lost a loved one. Her heart was sorrowful and her future bleak, for her only breadwinner had been removed by death. She discovered quickly that Jesus understood her deepest anguish; His grace lifted her burdens. It would be very difficult to believe His arrival at that precise moment was a thing of chance!

To remove a mistake (Matt. 15:21)

"Then Jesus went thence, and departed unto the coasts of Tyre and Sidon." As far as is known, this was a special visit to help a very needy family. A mother, a woman of Canaan, had a daughter who was grievously vexed with a devil. Modern science might describe the girl's condition as being an epileptic but, whatever men decide about her ailment, it remains obvious she needed constant attention. When the news arrived that Jesus was approaching the area, that Gentile woman conceived a plan by which she pretended to be a Jewess. Her confidence was quickly destroyed; but, when she admitted her guilt, the Lord graciously healed her child. Then, apparently, He returned from where He had come. It is unwise to be dogmatic about the exact movements of the Lord, but there is no record that He healed any other, and He didn't preach a sermon. (Compare vv. 28-29.)

To reach a maniac (Luke 8:26)

"And they arrived at the country of the Gadarenes." It is well known and irrefutable that, in close proximity to the land of the Gadarenes, were ten cities known as the Decapolis. However, there is no record to suggest Jesus ever visited that hillside again where, on that memorable day, He delivered a demoniac and saw 2,000 swine perish in the waters below the cliffs. The story is filled with drama, and it is easy to visualize the scene when the light of sanity began to show upon the face of the demoniac. The Lord planned that visit, and at a moment's notice clothed a naked man! There were no stores in the vicinity, so evidently Jesus came fully prepared to meet any emergency that might arise. He knew about that sufferer even before He met him.

To repeat a message (Luke 24:13-15)

"And, behold, two of them went that same day to a village called Emmaus . . . and . . . Jesus himself drew near, and went with them." Although Emmaus was in close proximity to Jerusalem, there is no record that Jesus had ever been there. When Christ was in the area, He spent much of His time either in the city or in Bethany, yet on this occasion the Lord apparently went out of His way to overtake two of His worried disciples. It would be wonderful if we could know all He uttered on that memorable journey. Doubtless He made the Scripture "come alive" as He expounded from ancient writings the things concerning Himself. What He said and did changed forever the lives of those who traveled with Him. He deliberately repeated what had frequently been uttered; He was alive, and death would never again terrorize His people.

To summarize all five of the preceding incidents, Jesus made special journeys to solve problems. The Bible states He is the same yesterday and today and forever. (See Heb. 13:8.) If He is the unchanging Christ, perhaps today He might make another journey to teach and help *us*.

A THREE-FOLD VIEW . . . of the art of giving

(JOHN 4:7; MATTHEW 25:8; 14:16)

The entire theme of the Bible may be expressed as *God giving to man.* The story of Bethlehem tells how God gave His Son to the world. The Gospels describe how Christ gave His message to the world. The resurrection tells how God provided hope and salvation for the world. God always did the giving; sinners were the recipients. Yet, as we examine the Scriptures more closely, it becomes evident that sometimes the order was reversed.

"Give me" (John 4:7) . . . *a disturbing surprise*

When the Lord made His special journey to Sychar's well, He knew He was about to meet one of the most infamous women in the city. Her moral virtues had disappeared, her presence was most undesirable, and even the normal chore of drawing water had to be done when other people were absent. To be caught in her presence invited gossip of the worst kind, and yet Jesus made a special effort to meet with her. His request for a drink occasioned surprise and led to one of the greatest of His accomplishments. She replied, "How is that thou, being a Jew, asketh drink of me, which am a woman of Samaria?" He answered: "If thou knewest the gift of God, and who it is that saith to thee, Give me to drink: thou wouldest have asked of him, and he would have given thee living water" (John 4:9-10). It appears to be strange that Christ should ask for a drink! Had He so desired, He could have given a command, and every drop of water in the well would have risen to quench His thirst. Was Jesus truly dependent upon the Samaritan? He had neither bucket nor rope, but the Lord of heaven would hardly have been helpless. He was trying to teach her — and us — that when we give to Him, He rewards us immeasurably. She gave water to Jesus; He gave *a well* to her.

"Give us" (Matthew 25:8) . . . *a desperate situation*

When the Savior spoke about the ten virgins, He enunciated truths of superlative worth. The disciples had asked about His return to earth, and consequently Jesus began to describe ten virgins who went forth to meet a bridegroom. Alas, five were wise and five were foolish. "They that were foolish took their lamps, and took no oil with them: But the wise took oil in their vessels with their lamps." The lamps used in those days were very small, and it was necessary to carry a flask or receptacle of some kind, which hung from a belt around the waist. When the bridegroom arrived unexpectedly, the ten young women arose hastily and, lighting their lamps, went forth to meet him. Within moments five lamps began to go out, and the virgins said to their companions, "Give us of your oil; for our lamps are gone out" (Matt. 25:3-8). Unfortunately, the wise virgins had no oil to spare, and the five foolish women lost their chance to attend the wedding. The picture that Christ presented revealed two things (1) The loss of the foolish virgins. (2) The bankruptcy of their companions. That they were able to enter with the bridegroom was a cause for rejoicing; but, had they remained awake, each one might have been a benefactor to her friend. It is necessary to remember that Jesus was describing conditions to precede His return. The need of the world would never be met unless the church — the wise ones — were in a position to respond when others asked for assistance.

"Give . . . them" (Matthew 14:16) . . . *a difficult suggestion*

The account that describes how Jesus fed five thousand men in addition to the women and children who accompanied them is probably one of the most exciting stories in the New Testament. It provides a reminder of the astonishing fact that the Savior was never anxious when an unexpected crisis arose. It was unbelievable that the Master should say, "Give ye them to eat." He was surely aware that the disciples had no spare supplies of food. They were speechless when He took five loaves and two fishes and performed a miracle. Did they understand that He was trying to teach them a great lesson? They could and would meet tremendous needs, but only after they had received supplies from His outstretched hand.

Christ's words spoken to the Samaritan woman may be summarized as "*How Unique.*" His story of the ten virgins may be expressed as "*How Urgent.*" The lessons taught in the account of the feeding of the multitude may be described "*How Unmistakable.*" Together they emphasize that what is given to Jesus is returned a thousandfold. Neither minister nor church can effectively meet the need of a dying world unless the Bread of Life is first received from the hand of the Savior. "Give, and it shall be given unto you; good measure, pressed down, and shaken together, and running over" (Luke 6:38).

An old minister said of the woman of Samaria that she left her pails and went away with the well [Christ]

THE CRIPPLE . . . who lived on the outside

(ACTS 3:2)

There have always been two types of people within the church; the *contented* and the *concerned.* Some received into church fellowship preferred to remain idle and were absent when anything special was being attempted for the Savior. Others never remained complacent and were possessed by desire to draw closer to Christ. They became indispensable and never needed coercion when helpers were needed to extend the kingdom of Christ. These types are as different as chalk is from cheese. The one lives on the outside begging; the other is found on the inside singing the praises of the Redeemer. The story of the cripple healed at the gate Beautiful of the temple supplies an illustration of these people.

The cripple . . . begging

Poor fellow! He had been lame from birth. It was very unfortunate, but he never had a triumphant beginning. The Bible says he was "lame from his mother's womb." There had been a malfunction in the formation of his body, and as a result he never experienced the joy of playing with other children. He was alive; he could see and understand what was being said but remained a cripple. Years later, either his family or friends carried him daily to the temple, where he became known to most of the worshipers who entered the sanctuary. His profession possibly became lucrative; not all beggars are poor! Every day he watched people entering the temple but apparently never shared their desire to worship. Maybe he heard the singing of the Levitical choir, but his soul was seldom thrilled. He lived on the outside. His hands were outstretched to beg and seldom lifted high in praise to God. The poor man thought only of getting; the idea of giving never entered his mind. He loved to see crowds of people approaching the sanctuary; their presence was good for business. He lived to count his coins!

The Christian . . . beholding

Seeing two men about to enter the temple, the beggar asked for alms. "Then Peter said, Silver and gold have I none; but such as I have give I thee: In the name of Jesus Christ of Nazareth rise up and walk." The contrast between the two men was obvious. The begger probably had money but craved for more; Peter had no money, but his heart overflowed with power money could not buy. It is worthy of attention that the donor of the new life for the cripple was not an angel who had descended from heaven but a sincere man who had recovered from humiliation and shame. The risen Christ had forgiven him, filled him with the Holy Spirit; and now, resplendent in righteousness, Peter was able to dispense healing to a helpless cripple at the gate. It is interesting to note that one man knelt in the dust outside; the other went to kneel in humility at the altar of God. Basically the cripple had nothing but money; Peter was a millionaire whose assets belonged to the Almighty. It is not difficult to decide which was the wealthier man.

The Christ . . . beholding

The cripple may have had a religion; the Christian had a Redeemer. The beggar had an intense desire to get; Peter had a greater desire to give. The beggar might have said, "God helps those who help themselves." Peter would have replied, "They alone are truly helped who know how to seek first the kingdom of God." The beggar owed no man anything, except perhaps the people who carried him daily to and fron the temple; he was probably a very shrewd business man. Peter and John were conscious of a debt that could never be repaid, a debt of gratitude to Christ, who had redeemed them from the power and slavery of sin. The cripple could not beg enough money; they could not get enough of their Lord! The benediction from heaven constantly enriched the Christians, but the continual begging did nothing for the cripple's feet! Nevertheless, when the poor man came into contact with Christ's men, his outlook changed forever. "And he leaping up stood, and walked, and entered with them into the temple, walking, and leaping, and praising God." Unless another beggar claimed his place at the gate Beautiful of the temple, his seat remained empty forever. There are lessons in the ancient story that modern Christians need to learn. It is always better to have a full heart within the temple than to have a full pocket and a bankrupt soul outside. "If ye then be risen with Christ, *seek those things which are above*, where Christ sitteth on the right hand of God" (Col. 3:1). This is an account of the beggar, the believer, and the blessing. It might be wise to ask where we fit into the story.

THREE QUEENS . . . with a problem

The old addage, "If in doubt, don't," is not the wisest statement made by men. There are times when necessity demands immediate action, when procrastination is the deadliest enemy of the soul. Three women mentioned in the Scripture provide evidence to support this assertion.

The woman who remained indifferent (Acts 24:24)

Concerning Drusilla, the very beautiful wife of Felix, Adam Clark has written the following: "About the year of our Lord 53, Agrippa married her to Azizus, king of the Emesenes, who received her on condition of being circumcised. Felix, having seen her, fell desperately in love with her, and by means of a pretending Jewish magician, a native of Cyprus, persuaded her to leave her husband, on which Felix took her to wife. She appears to have been a woman of indifferent character, though one of the finest women of that age. It is said that she, and a son she had by Felix, were consumed in an eruption of Vesuvius." It has been estimated that, at the time of her appearance before Paul, she was a young woman of eighteen years. She was a Jewess whose behavior was condemned by Hebrew law.

When she and her husband listened to the preaching of Paul, her conscience must have been stirred. The prisoner reasoned of righteousness, self control, and judgment to come; and the message convicted them. Both Felix and his wife were immoral. They lived to satisfy their passions, and the encounter with a preacher of righteousness challenged their attitude. When Felix trembled and said, "Go thy way *for this time*; when I have a convenient season I will call for thee," he had other designs on the apparently helpless prisoner. "He hoped also that money should have been given him of Paul, that he might loose him: wherefore he sent for him the oftener, and communed with him" (Acts 24:25-27). The woman doubtless shared her husband's decision. She remained indifferent to what God had said; she would please herself and become rich in the process!

The woman who really investigated (1 Kings 10:1)

"And when the queen of Sheba heard of the fame of Solomon concerning the name of the LORD, she came to prove him with hard questions." Later she said, "It was a true report that I heard in mine own land of thy acts and of thy wisdom. Howbeit I believed not the words, until I came, and mine eyes had seen it: and, behold, the half was not told me: thy wisdom and prosperity exceedeth the fame which I heard" (vv. 6-7). Jesus called this lady "The queen of the south" (Matt. 12:42) and commended the wisdom that brought her from the uttermost parts of the earth. Her kingdom was in Arabia, and her journey was indeed a long one judged by the size of the world as it was known in those times. She could not live with her doubts. She wanted to know what could be known, and any demands that might be made upon her private life were of little importance. This lady may not have possessed the rare beauty of Drusilla, but she certainly had more intelligence.

The woman who respectfully interceded (Esth. 8:4)

Unlike the Queen of Sheba, who had never met Solomon, Esther loved and married her king. However, certain rigid laws within the kingdom of Ahasuerus made it necessary for all ladies, including the queen, to remain at a distance. To approach the throne without being summoned was an offense. Vashti, the former queen who refused to be paraded before the lustful eyes of assembled guests, lost her throne because of rash disobedience. Even women of high rank were the slaves of their husbands. The story told in the Book of Esther is exceedingly interesting. It never mentions God by name, but His presence is felt throughout its chapters. Intrigue, suspicion, hatred, and danger threatened God's people; and, finally, Esther was asked to place her life in jeopardy that the Hebrews might be spared. This young woman learned how to pray. No thoughtful reader could ever doubt that, although the formal petition was placed before Ahasuerus, her real prayer ascended to the throne of the King of Kings. Her intercession saved a nation, and her exploits will never be forgotten.

There appears to be a vast difference between the Queen of Sheba and Esther. The lady from Sheba came to Solomon, admired the wisdom he displayed, but afterward returned to her land to live on memories. Esther not only loved her king but saw him often; and, because of her rich fellowship with the monarch, many people were blessed immeasurably. These queens provide a startling contrast and illustrate two types of Christians. Some appear to be content with the initial contact. They praise the Lord, present certain gifts, but afterward live at a distance! Others linger in the King's presence to share His heart and table. Of the women mentioned here, which would we most resemble?

PAUL . . . who was always ready

One of the most important words in the Bible is "ready." It was often used by the Savior and obviously became the standard by which Paul measured the effectiveness of his life and ministry. To be ready implied that the person concerned had made adequate preparation for any eventuality. It has been recorded that Nehemiah's builders held a tool in one hand and a weapon in the other. They were ready either to build or fight. The same situation exists on the northern boundaries of modern Israel. The young men work in the fields, but carry machine guns. They are ready either to defend their homeland or develop it. Paul was that type of man, and the statement "I am ready" may be found in several places throughout his writings.

"I am ready to preach" . . . his powerful testimony (Rom. 1:15)

This section of his testimony may be summarized under three headings: His *Concern, Courage*, and *Challenge*. Paul believed he had been given the gospel for Gentile hearers. It was therefore his duty to do as he had been commanded. To retain something that belonged to others was a theft. Unless he delivered his message, he would be illegally holding something not his. He emphasized: "I am debtor both to the Greeks, and to the Barbarians" (Rom. 1:14) and went on to say, "So, as much as in me is, I am ready to preach the gospel to you that are at Rome also." Rome was a place of great opportunity, but it also presented continual danger. Some preachers would have stayed in safer places! To many, it would have seemed suicidal to preach in a city where Caesar favored the execution of heretics! Paul never avoided danger; he flung caution to the winds and often went where others never ventured. He stated that the fame of the Roman church was known throughout the world, and it would be a privilege if he were able to speak with its members — especially those of "Caesar's household." His constant readiness to witness anywhere and at any time should be an example for all preachers.

"I am ready to come to you" . . . his painful testing (2 Cor. 12:14-15)

"The more abundantly I love you, the less I am loved." Corinth was one of the most sinful cities of ancient times. Idols were worshiped, moral filth was commonplace, and people lived to satisfy their lustful nature. Paul had remained there for eighteen months, and a flourishing church had been formed. Presented with an increasing opportunity to evangelize the area, the local Christians had failed in their obligations and finally devoted time to the criticism of the man to whom, under God, they owed everything. They compared him with the original twelve apostles and rejected his claim to be their equal. It may never be known to what extent this hurt the apostle; the wounds inflicted upon his soul were deep and painful. Yet, ignoring the insults and insinuations, Paul wrote to the church to say, "Behold, the third time I am ready to come to you. . . . And I will very gladly spend and be spent for you." This forgiving attitude possibly expressed one of his greatest achievements. It is very difficult to admire unappreciative brethren! It is not easy to be kind to false friends! Paul was a great saint, and that explains why God blessed him.

"I am ready . . . to die" . . . his personal tragedy (Acts 21:13)

The church was troubled! Philip, the evangelist, was gravely concerned, for something was wrong, and every member of the local assembly had become apprehensive. Paul, their illustrious visitor, was determined to proceed to Jerusalem, and everybody believed he was making a mistake. The brethren who resided at Tyre had said to Paul "*through the Spirit, that he should not go up to Jerusalem*" (Acts 21:4), but they wasted their time. The apostle had made up his mind, and nothing would turn him from his self-appointed path. When Agabus, a prophet from Judea, arrived to take Paul's girdle and bind his own hands and feet and say, "*Thus saith the Holy Ghost*, So shall the Jews at Jerusalem bind the man that owneth this girdle," the listeners became very fearful. "Then Paul answered, What mean ye to weep and to break mine heart? for I am ready not to be bound only, but also to die at Jerusalem for the name of the Lord Jesus" (Acts 21:11-13). Unfortunately, Paul refused to obey God's command and, as a result, lost two years of his life. Instead of preaching to precious souls, he languished in a prison at Jerusalem. Yet, even in his mistake, it is possible to recognize the unrelenting courage of a man who refused to avoid danger.

"I am now ready to be offered" . . . his permanent triumph (2 Tim. 4:6)

Years had passed; Paul had learned his lesson and was seated in a Roman prison. The end of his earthly pilgrimage was approaching. Calm and unafraid, the great apostle contemplated his future. Writing to Timothy he said, "*I am now ready to be offered.*" With three dynamic sentences, he summarized his ministry. "I have fought a good fight, I have finished my course, I have kept the faith." He wrote of his *fight, finish*, and *faith.* He had never been a dropout! His future was bright with prospect and hope. "Henceforth there is laid up for me a crown of righteousness, which the Lord . . . shall give me" (4:8). Paul had always been ready to serve his Master; now he was ready to meet Him face to face. Blessed is the man or woman who shares that glorious confidence!

PAUL . . . and the source of his spiritual wealth . . . "In whom we have"

The apostle Paul was probably the greatest evangelist of all time. His service to the church was of incalculable worth. Although he had very little money, he was perhaps the wealthiest of all Christians — not in earthly assets, but in spiritual power. This outstanding fact is clearly seen in his letter to the Ephesians.

In Christ we have redemption through His blood . . . pardon (Eph. 1:7)

It is noteworthy that most of the inhabitants of Ephesus were Gentiles who were worshipers of the goddess Diana. Their city had been notoriously sinful, but the gospel so transformed the district that, before the end of the second century, all its citizens had become Christians. It would have been expected that Jews would understand the message of redemption through the blood of sacrifice, but for pagans to accept this truth testifies to the effectiveness of Paul's ministry. He did not hesitate to speak about the atoning death of the Lord Jesus, for he knew that for all people this alone was the power of God unto salvation. It is thrilling to read Paul's words: " . . . the forgiveness of sins, according to the riches of his grace." God's grace is marvelous, but the apostle spoke of *the riches* of His grace. That indicates grace in all its fullness. Pardon given to undeserving sinners is measured by the infinite grace of a compassionate God.

In Christ we have an inheritance . . . provision (Eph. 1:11)

An inheritance is something claimed after the donor has died! The writer to the Hebrews said: "For where a testament is, there must also of necessity be the death of the testator. For a testament is of force after men are dead; otherwise it is of no strength at all while the testator liveth" (Heb. 9:16-17). It was the desire of the Lord that redeemed sinners should receive an inheritance to supply their need through time and eternity. This was only made possible when the Testator's death validated His will. Later, in the Epistle to the Ephesians, Paul itemized the details of the provision made by the Prince of heaven.

In Christ we have been sealed . . . possessed (Eph. 1:13)

So that there could be no mistake in the identity of claimants to this eternal fortune, the stamp of ownership was placed on every believer. That the Christian was eligible to receive an inheritance could never be challenged or questioned in a court of law; the stamp of heaven was indelibly placed on his soul. Paul said, "Ye were sealed with that holy Spirit of promise.'' Many logging companies fell trees in the Canadian forests, but these are immediately stamped with the special mark of the owner. The logs thereafter float down rivers to the lake where they are examined and separated. There is never a problem of identity for each log ''is sealed'' with a stamp of ownership. Christians may mingle with millions of other human beings; but, sealed by the Holy Spirit, their identity can never be confused.

In Christ we have become a habitation . . . privilege (Eph. 3:22)

Paul went to great lengths to explain that, within the fellowship of the church, racial bitterness should be nonexistent. Jews and Gentiles were united. Old barriers had been removed to create God's substitute for the temple at Jerusalem. Formerly it was claimed Jehovah lived in the sanctuary made by men; Paul affirmed something new had been created. Christians had become a home for the indwelling Spirit of God. (See 1 Cor. 3:16.)

In Christ we have boldness . . . pleasure (Eph. 3:12)

This was no ''flash in the pan'' doctrine, something about which to argue, something which might be proven false. It was ''According to the eternal purpose which [God] purposed in Christ Jesus'' (v. 11). What had been planned in eternity had been accomplished in time. Paul was absolutely sure of the provisions in his inheritance and said that every believer should share his confidence. Neither shame nor hesitancy should be evident when the believer stated his case before men. There could be no doubt about the realities claimed; God had endorsed what had been said.

In Christ we have access . . . permission (Eph. 3:12)

Access into the ancient Holy of Holies had been denied to all except the high priest of Israel. He had been permitted, once a year, to go beyond the veil to stand at the mercy seat. All prohibitions have now been swept away by the death of Christ. Jesus opened a new and living way to the heart of the Father, and all who desire can ''come boldly unto the throne of grace, that we may obtain mercy, and find grace to help in time of need.'' (See Heb. 4:16.) Paul was a wealthy believer, but we also may claim an identical inheritance . . . if we know how!

PAUL . . . who had firm convictions

Paul was a preacher with deep convictions; this was made evident in his Epistle to the Galatians. "I marvel that ye are so soon removed from him that called you into the grace of Christ unto another gospel: which is not another. . . . But though we, or an angel from heaven, preach any other gospel unto you than that which we have preached unto you, let him be accursed. As we have said before, so say I now again, If any other man preach any other gospel unto you than that ye have received, let him be accursed" (Gal. 1:6-9). This was the strongest possible language Paul could have used, for actually he was saying any other message would condemn the preacher eternally. To understand the details of Paul's faith, it is necessary to study his letter to the Ephesians, for there, using the word "without," Paul clearly expressed what he believed.

Without Christ . . . having no hope; and without God (Eph. 2:12)

Paul reminded his readers what they once were. He had arrived in Ephesus to preach to people who worshiped the goddess Diana, he had stayed two years, and the grace of God had saved many souls. It was incomprehensible to Paul that any who had heard the glorious message of Christ could ever deny their faith or lose their first love for Jesus. There were good, sincere citizens in Ephesus, and some of them might have been living exemplary lives. Yet Paul insisted that, however good they were, they remained lost and without hope. Unless Jesus Christ, who claimed to be the only way to the true God, was accepted as Savior, no person in Ephesus or anywhere else could enter the kingdom of God. Paul maintained that good works were insufficient, that without Christ people were in danger of eternal damnation.

We appear to have reached an age where this kind of preaching has vanished. It has become customary not to offend listeners. There is good in all men, so we have been told, and the duty of the church is to locate that good and encourage it. It is to help people climb the ladder of morality and find acceptance with a very understanding God. Paul would have argued furiously against such conclusions. He believed that men at their best were still lost and vehemently said so.

Without blame before Him in love (Eph. 1:4)

Paul reminded his readers that "We all had our conversation in times past in the lusts of our flesh, fulfilling the desires of the flesh and of the mind; and were by nature the children of wrath, even as others. But God, who is rich in mercy, for his great love wherewith he loved us, Even when we were dead in sins, hath quickened us together with Christ. . . . That in the ages to come he might show the exceeding riches of his grace in his kindness toward us through Christ Jesus'' (Eph. 2:3-7). With that end in view, Paul said every Christian should endeavor to cooperate with the Lord in striving to be ''without blame.'' This suggested a victorious life with the power of indwelling sin overcome and the Holy Spirit permitted to occupy every part of the human temple. This meant growth in grace.

Without blemish . . . a glorious church (Eph. 5:27)

Someone has said, ''*Christianity is a life of new beginnings.*'' Paul appears to stress that our walk with the risen Christ leads to higher and better accomplishments. Having rescued us from the power of sin, Christ continues His work until the entire church will be perfected. Paul urges husbands to love their wives and wives similarly to love and honor their husbands. Christian homes would then reflect the love of the Almighty. Discord, envy, strife, and bitterness should have no part in any heart or home. Each day should take believers closer to that glorious culmination when, without blemish, the church will be presented faultless to the heavenly Bridegroom. The sanctity of marriage was something never to be forgotten. Divorce could never be a reflection of the love of Christ for His church. Therefore, the Ephesians were reminded of the need to exercise love in every facet of family life, for only thus would the world be attracted to the ways of Christianity.

Unfortunately, something appears to have gone wrong with the modern church. The old ideals of family dedication, in many instances, have vanished; people get married in haste and repent at leisure. It can only be a cause for regret when marriages terminate because a man or woman permits the entrance of illegitimate interests. People who have responded to Christ should be without blame; only thus can the church be perfected. Is it possible that we could be thwarting the purposes of God?

PAUL . . . who liked the word "glorious"

Scientists recently said that, if reactors were placed in the Australian desert, they would generate enough power from the sun to meet all the energy needs of the United States of America. Our minds cannot comprehend the magnitude of this fact, for the sun is said to be 93 million miles from the planet earth. Its scintillating radiance can only be matched by the glory of God. Maybe this astonishing fact influenced Paul in his choice of words. He used many adjectives, but it appears from his writings his favorite expression was "glorious."

The glorious gospel of the blessed God (1 Tim. 1:11 and 2 Cor. 4:4)

"The god of this world hath blinded the minds of them which believe not, lest the light of the glorious gospel of Christ, who is the image of God, should shine unto them." There is special significance in the fact that these words were written to the church at Corinth. That seaport city had become infamous for its corruption. Paul established a church there, and the grace of God had been manifested among very guilty people. Idols were destroyed, confessions made, and the precious blood of Christ washed away their sins. Christ was presented as being "the very image of God;" that is, the Son and the Father were so alike it was impossible to tell them apart! God had sent good news that, through the death of Christ, all men could be forgiven. This was a glorious tiding.

The glorious liberty of the children of God (Rom. 8:21)

"The creature itself also shall be delivered from the bondage of corruption into *the glorious liberty of the children of God.*" The contrast as expressed in this verse is enormous. "The bondage of corruption" is compared to the liberty found in Christ. The laws of Moses had set standards of excellence but left people unable to reach the exalted ideals. Heathenism had little to offer except bondage. Both for Jew and Gentile the outlook had been ominous, for all were slaves of sin. Jesus said, "If the Son therefore shall make you free, ye shall be free indeed" (John 8:36). The liberating power of the gospel united Jew and Gentile, freemen and slaves, rich and poor, old and young, educated and illiterate, and made them members of the family of the living God.

The glorious body of the risen Christ (Phil. 3:21)

"We look for the Savior, the Lord Jesus Christ: Who shall change our vile body, that it may be fashioned like unto his glorious body." The end of mortality is death; the termination of life brings people to a grave! God's plan is to give to His children an incorruptible body. The body in which Jesus lived for over thirty years was still the same after His resurrection, but it had been changed, for the mortal had put on immortality. Although He carried the nailprints in His hands, He was still able to eat food before His doubtful followers.

The glorious church (Eph. 5:27)

"Christ also loved the church, and gave himself for it . . . that he might present it to himself a glorious church, not having spot, or wrinkle, or any such thing" (vv. 25, 27). The formation of a united company of believers was one of the greatest projects ever undertaken by God. Racial barriers were to be abolished, enmities would be destroyed, and all men would become brethren. Furthermore, it was the Lord's intention to transform and beautify that assembly until all its members became completely Christlike. John exclaimed triumphantly, "When he shall appear, we shall be like him" (1 John 3:2). There will be many wonders in heaven, but one of the brightest stars to shine in eternity will be "the Lamb's bride, clothed in fine linen, the righteousness of saints." She will be resplendent in holiness — a glorious church.

The glorious appearing (Titus 2:13-14)

"Looking for the blessed hope, and the glorious appearing of the great God and our Savior Jesus Christ: Who gave himself for us, that he might redeem us from all iniquity." Paul apparently used his favorite word to express convictions about every facet of the Christian life. From the beginning to the end of God's plan of salvation, everything was glorious! Nothing he could imagine could compare with the thrilling event when the Savior would descend in the clouds of heaven to save His people and establish a kingdom of righteousness. Then, "The wolf also shall dwell with the lamb, and the leopard shall lie down with the kid; and the calf and the young lion and the fatling together; and a little child shall lead them" (Isa. 11:6). Paul was convinced that everything about the gospel was glorious — he was correct in his assessment.

PAUL . . . who might have written the Epistle to the Hebrews

There has been much debate concerning the identity of the person who wrote the Epistle to the Hebrews. The letter is different from any other book in the New Testament. Theologians cite Barnabas, Apollos, and other lesser-known men, but available evidence is inadequate to prove any of the ideas expressed in scholastic circles. Those who favor Pauline authorship state the book expressed the training that Saul received in the school of Gamaliel. They further emphasize that the Epistle to the Hebrews represents the way in which Paul preached the gospel to synagogue audiences. Others state the language used by Paul was similar to that used in the letter to the Hebrews. Even this is inconclusive. If a speaker admires another, it often becomes evident that the methods, mannerisms, idiosyncrasies, and words are unwittingly assimilated into the admirer's presentation. His works then exhibit a striking resemblance to those of the admired friend. This may be detected in the three "much mores" of this study.

The "much more" of grace (Heb. 9:14)

The Epistle to the Hebrews resembles an art gallery where ancient and modern pictures are contrasted and compared. The Old Testament practices are compared with the new; the ancient offerings, with the sacrifice of the Savior. The blood of animals is contrasted with the precious blood of the Lamb of God, and it becomes obvious that the author had an intimate knowledge of the temple, its customs, feasts, offerings, and demands. Apollos, who had a great knowledge of the Scriptures (see Acts 18:24), could easily have written the book, but the same possibility applies to Paul. Throughout the Pauline letters reference is made to the "much more" of many things. It represented force of argument. "If the blood of bulls and of goats . . . sanctifieth to the purifying of the flesh: How *much more* shall the blood of Christ . . . purge your conscience?" (9:13-14). Actually there is hardly a comparison. The blood of animals merely supplied a *covering* for sin; the blood of Jesus removes it eternally. The glorious redemption found in Christ, the manifestation of the grace of God, exceeded anything known in the history of the human race. The ancient worshipers bought their sacrifice; Jesus was supplied by God and is free to all who accept Him.

The "much more" of growth (Rom. 5:10)

Paul wrote: "For if, when we were enemies, we were reconciled to God by the death of his Son, *much more*, being reconciled, we shall be saved by his life.'' The first four chapters in the letter to the Romans express Paul's doctrine concerning lost sinners. Having wandered from God; having become sinners — slaves — enemies, they were in danger of eternal judgment. But Christ appeared to put away sin by the sacrifice of Himself, and forgiveness became possible for all who believe in the Lamb of God. Paul argued that much time and labor had been spent on reclaiming perishing sinners. The task had to be completed, or what had been done earlier would be a waste of time and effort. When a potter discovered grit or unyielding substances in his clay, he did not discard the materials. He broke the vessel, removed the hindrances, and proceeded to complete what had been commenced. Paul considered the Lord to be the Master Potter. Since he had done so much for His believing people, it was incumbent upon the Savior to complete His task. His ''much more'' of grace brought people to the bottom of God's mountain. The ''much more'' of growth revealed the way by which the Guide would get Christians to the top of that mountain.

The ''much more'' of guilt (Heb. 12:25)

''See that ye refuse not him that speaketh. For if they escaped not who refused him that spake on earth, ''much more'' shall not we escape, if we turn away from him that speaketh from heaven.'' The gospel spoke about a greater message, a greater salvation, through a greater High Priest. Hebrews 6:4-6 warns of guilt for which God had no remedy. People who knew the truth, but rejected it because they refused to leave their sin, could not expect mercy in the hereafter. To sin against the light was to sign one's death certificate. There could be no forgiveness for a person who ''trampled under foot the Son of God.'' That was the greater guilt, the unpardonable sin mentioned in the New Testament. It was the most urgent warning given in the Word of God. Wise men listen and learn; only fools laugh!

THE FIRST HIGHWAY THROUGH HEBREWS
. . . "Jesus is better"

The Epistle to the Hebrews was written to people whose world seemed to be disintegrating. They were Jews who had been attracted to Christianity but, unfortunately, had not forsaken Judaism. When the temple was destroyed, when the daily sacrifices ceased to be offered, and when priests no longer ministered, all appeared to be deathblows to converts. The writer of this letter tried to prove that, in spite of the catastrophies that overwhelmed the nation, all was not lost. The new faith in Christ offered far better things than those that had been lost. The word "better" is a key word in the epistle.

Jesus is better than angels (Heb. 1:4)

The author begins with the deity of Christ. Earthly calamities fade into insignificance in the light of the supreme majesty of the Son of God. Attention is drawn to the tremendous statement in 1:8: "But unto the Son he saith, Thy throne, O God, is for ever and ever: a sceptre of righteousness is the sceptre of thy kingdom." Having dealt with the problem of sin, the Savior had been seated at the right hand of God's throne. This was an unassailable fact, and the Hebrews were instructed to consider this as the basis for all further thought.

Jesus is better than priests (Heb. 7:7)

Explaining how Christ was a priest after the order of Melchizedek, the writer went on to explain that the ancient priest had ministered many years before the birth of Aaron and that, since Abraham gave tithes to the illustrious king of Salem, his descendants — in him — did likewise (v. 9). All the priests who descended from Abraham were limited in their efforts. They could never complete what they commenced, for death ultimately terminated their ministry. Jesus was therefore greater than they. The Aaronic priesthood had disappeared; Christ would remain eternally.

Jesus represented a better hope (Heb. 7:19)

The laws of Moses, in which the Jews trusted, could only condemn. They told men what to do but then condemned them for their inability to keep the commandments. The law outlined a road to be traveled but left men with paralyzed feet! The "better hope," as revealed in the gospel, gave to recipients power to accomplish the impossible! The law had been a schoolmaster to bring students to the better Teacher . . . Jesus.

Jesus presented a better testament (Heb. 7:22; 8:6)

The promises — the inheritance to be found in Christ — superceded anything ever known by the forefathers. They were superior to anything within the law. Old Testament saints knew nothing of the indwelling power of the Holy Spirit. They were unaware of the peace obtained through the shed blood of the Redeemer. The prophets spoke about the possibility of obtaining eternal wealth, but Jesus supplied it!

Jesus had been a better sacrifice (Heb. 9:23)

It was not difficult to understand how the sacrifice of the Son of God was superior to the sacrifice of a turtle dove, lamb, or a bullock. An Old Testament offering *covered* sin; Christ *banished* it forever. The former system spoke of an offering for a family; Jesus became the Lamb of God who took away the sins of the whole world. The prophets spoke of "the blood of the lamb," but the Christians could speak of the *precious* blood of the Lamb. This was a *better* message.

Jesus was a better substance (Heb. 10:34)

The early Christians endured much hardship, but they triumphed because they knew their citizenship was in heaven. They dealt with eternal realities and were fully assured of their ultimate destination. They were not hoping to receive everlasting life; they already had it!

Jesus represented a better country (Heb. 11:16)

Abraham had gone forth searching for a city whose builder and maker was God. Yet every earthly country was filled with danger. Jesus had gone to prepare mansions in eternity — He said so. (See John 14:2.) The future of the saints was bright with prospect and hope.

Jesus promised a better resurrection (Heb. 11:35)

Chapter 11 describes Old Testament saints who had endured torture as they prayed for deliverance from death. Jesus was the fulfillment of their dreams. He said, "He that believeth in me . . . shall never die" (John 11: 25-26). This was truly a glorious highway through Hebrews.

THE SECOND HIGHWAY THROUGH HEBREWS ... "Let us"

It must be remembered that this highway is the natural extension of the first. Having mentioned the better things to be found in the Christian way of living, the author goes on to indicate milestones along the road that lead to the fullness of the blessing of God. Highway 1 was a map showing ways of travel through a territory; highway 2 reveals the traveler beginning to make progress toward a desired destination! The writer makes an impassioned appeal to his readers to put into practice the things heard.

Let us therefore fear (Heb. 4:1)

(See also 3:1-11.) The author reminds his readers that in former generations the people of God possessed much knowledge and yet failed to enter the Promised Land. Hebrews 6:4 stresses this fact. The hesitant people to whom this letter was sent appeared to be in similar danger. They knew truth but remained reluctant to accept its demands.

Let us labor (Heb. 4:11)

There was urgent need for these people to arise and with boldness do something. If dangers threatened, they were to be courageous and overcome them. The time had arrived to act and not talk. Nothing could be of more importance than entering into the kingdom of God.

Let us hold fast (Heb. 4:14)

(Compare Rev. 3:11.) Those wavering, hesitant people needed to hold fast, for otherwise the most precious commodities in this world and the next might be lost. Wise people give consideration to the questions: "How best can a man or woman hold fast the things of God? What are the greatest assets of the believer? What is the secret of successful living for Christ?"

Let us come boldly (Heb. 4:16)

Nothing can ever be an effective substitute for communion with God. The man who seldom meets his Lord has no chance of success. Service for God is excellent, but worship is better. Service may indicate the light is shining, but worship charges the batteries! The man who never prays is like a plant without water.

Let us go on (Heb. 6:1)

The Christian who never grows in grace cannot be effective for his Lord; the man who knows everything knows nothing! Knowledge is thought to be the ultimate asset. That cannot be correct. To be *like* Christ is far better than knowing about Him. Instead of looking for blemishes in brethren, eyes should be focused on the great High Priest who ever lives to make intercession for us.

Let us consider one another (Heb. 10:24)

The church is a fellowship of those who love Christ; it is a family of people like ourselves. Occasionally problems arise within the assembly. Understanding is better than criticism; love is better than tension. A person without compassion is a poor example of the Lord who loved everybody.

Let us run with patience (Heb. 12:1)

Christians resemble athletes in a stadium. The grandstands are filled with spectators — maybe spectators from unseen worlds. No runner would burden himself by running with weights around his neck. He avoids every hindrance, and Christians performing in life's marathon should emulate that example. They should lay aside every weight and the sin that so easily besets them and run patiently the race. The Galatians ran well for a time but were hindered; we must not make the same mistake. (See Gal. 3:1.)

Let us go forth (Heb. 13:13)

To follow in the footsteps of Christ, it is necessary to avoid the world with its insidious temptations and alluring attractions. Peter denied the Lord when he sought fellowship and warmth at the enemies' fire. We must, therefore, "Go forth" to Him "without the camp." Separated Christians have a greater chance of becoming consecrated Christians. We must be in the world, but not of it!

Let us offer praise (Heb. 13:15)

The greatest advertisement for Christ and the gospel is a happy, radiant believer. Scowls, complaints, criticisms, and sorrowful expressions are not reflections of overflowing happiness. If God has been gracious and good to us, we should give thanks to Him. Faith is like a mockingbird . . . it sings in the dark.

THE THIRD HIGHWAY THROUGH HEBREWS . . . Jesus is able

Hebrews 5:7 is possibly one of the most thought-provoking statements in the Bible; it refers to the only occasion when Christ "feared." It belongs to that memorable occasion when, in the Garden of Gethsemane, Jesus fought for His life. (Read Luke 22:40-44.) The cup to which the Lord made reference was that of human weakness. Satan was trying to kill the Lord prematurely. Jesus, realizing His life was being threatened, prayed to be saved from death, and His prayer was answered when the angel came to strengthen Him.

Jesus was able to save (Heb. 7:25)

To infer that the humanity of Jesus desired a way by which to avoid going to Calvary, is *not* correct. Jesus was the Lamb slain from the foundation of the world. He came to earth to die. When He contemplated "the death of the cross," He did so with increasing joy. (See Heb. 12:1-2.) The verse mentioned at the beginning of this section enables readers to understand to what depths of suffering and shame He went to provide salvation for sinners. What happened in the Garden of Gethsemane and on the green hill revealed He came to save lost souls, and the first phase of the operation had been successfully concluded. The way was now open to make real in human experience that which had been planned in eternity. His sacrificial death on the cross had atoned for sin; His precious blood could obliterate human guilt; forgiveness had become gloriously possible. The author of this epistle was quite sure that Jesus was not only able to save; He was able to continue the work until every person had been transformed into the image of God's Son.

Jesus was able to succour (Heb. 2:18; 4:15)

It must always be remembered that this letter was sent to people who were in real trouble. Their problems were not imaginary! Some were suffering from severe persecution; some were even dying. It was difficult for them to embrace a new faith when their God appeared indifferent to human need. (Read 4:15, and consider the "touched.") The word from which this was derived means "to sympathize." The rendering should be: "For we have not an high priest who is [unable to sympathize] with the feeling of our infirmities; but [He] was in all points tempted like as we are, yet without sin." The author insisted that Jesus, having walked our pathway in life, was not only aware of our problems but was, out of His own experience, able to understand and supply that for which weary souls yearned. This simple but glorious fact connects the second highway with the third. In view of the truth that Jesus had become our High Priest, all His followers should "therefore come boldly unto the throne of grace, that we may obtain mercy, and find grace to help in time of need." (See 4:16.) As a mother comforts her child, so the Lord could comfort and sustain His children.

Jesus was able to sanctify (Heb. 7:25)

The salvation offered in Christ was more than the forgiveness of sin. Read 1 John 3:2 and realize that all converts must be made like Christ, as there can be no imperfection in heaven. It was because our High Priest — unlike the members of the Aaronic priesthood — would never die; He will be able to complete that which He began. His intercession for us at God's right hand, is the guarantee that He will never "give up" on His difficult task. However, it is vitally necessary that we "come unto God by him." Only thus can God's plan succeed. We must cooperate in His endeavor. Having started a process, the Lord desired to complete it. Having lifted sinners *from the uttermost*, He intended to save them *to the uttermost.*

These three themes from the Epistle to the Hebrews appear as milestones on the third highway through the book. The Hebrews were urged not to be content with lesser goals and not to exist in the valley of doubt and despondency when it was possible to climb into mountains of spiritual experience and enjoy the sunshine of God's favor. Things were better and brighter ahead, and nothing should ever be permitted to ruin the ongoing, uplifting experience of walking and climbing with God. As John Bunyan explained in his book, *The Pilgrim's Progress,* we came from the city of destruction but our final destination is the celestial city, where there is no need of the sun. With the poet we should sing:

> I'm pressing on the upward way,
> New heights I'm gaining every day;
> Still praying as I'm onward bound,
> "Lord, plant my feet on higher ground."

THE FOURTH HIGHWAY THROUGH HEBREWS . . . this Man, the incomparable Christ

The theme of this great epistle is the incomparable Christ, the High Priest of His people. He was born in a stable but has since thrilled kings and queens in palaces. He never attended any university, but He has engaged the attention of every scholar on earth. He never had an army, but He has conquered the world. He seldom handled money, but He possessed something money could never buy. This epistle reveals Him in a very unique manner.

This man and Moses (Heb. 3:3)

"For this man was counted worthy of more glory than Moses, inasmuch as he who hath builded the house hath more honour than the house." Moses was a servant in the household of God; Jesus was the eternal Son. He belonged in the intimate circles of the divine fellowship. The first chapter stresses the fact that the worlds were made by Him; He had been appointed heir of all things. The revered lawgiver of Israel could not even compare with the description given in Hebrews 1:3: "Who being the brightness of his glory, and the express image of his person, and upholding all things by the word of his power, when he had by himself purged our sins, sat down on the right hand of the Majesty on high" (Heb. 1:3). Moses was born among captives in Egypt; Jesus, the Son of God, existed before time began; He inhabited eternity. This *Man* was truly magnificent and completely incomparable.

This man and the priests (Heb. 7:23-24)

The entire nation of Israel had for centuries placed their trust in the Aaronic priesthood. Once every year the high priest entered within the veil to represent people before the mercy seat. It seemed inconceivable that the nation could exist without such aid. When this ministry terminated, everyone was overwhelmed with grief and despair. This epistle explained that the seeming catastrophe was of little consequence. Even Aaron's ministry had been limited. He could not complete what he commended. "And they truly were many priests, because they were not suffered to continue by reason of death. But *this man*, because he continueth ever, hath an unchangeable priesthood." Furthermore, Jesus was not only a Priest, He was a *royal Priest.* Citing the ancient Melchizedek as an example, this author went on to expound the glorious fact that the Lord was a Priest after that royal order. His love guaranteed that He would represent sinners, but His power guaranteed He would be able to bring relief to the supplicant. See also the earlier study in this book. Melchizedek . . . who never had any parents!

This man and His offering (Heb. 8:3)

It was required that every Old Testament priest offer sacrifices, for "without shedding of blood is no remission" (Heb. 9:22). Yet *no priest* ever offered his own blood! To do such a thing would have been useless and blasphemous. The Lord was supremely unique. "Neither by the blood of goats and calves, but by *his own blood* he entered in once into the holy place, having obtained eternal redemption for us" (Heb. 9:12). Christ was different! The merits of His precious blood easily surpassed the blood of turtledoves, lambs, and bullocks. The termination of the Aaronic priesthood was of little consequence. Christians had a better priest, who offered a better sacrifice. This High Priest lived to make intercession for us. He was complete in every aspect of His ministry. Nevertheless, to enhance that ministry, we must cooperate with Him, by drawing near in "full assurance of faith" (Heb. 10:22).

This man and His expectancy (Heb. 10:12-13)

"But this man, after he had offered one sacrifice for sins for ever, sat down on the right hand of God; From henceforth expecting till his enemies be made his footstool." (1) *How different*! There was never another like Him. (2) *How decisive*! He offered *one sacrifice* — not many; *for ever* — not just a limited period of time. (3) *How deliberate*! He sat down! There was neither panic nor haste. With absolute dignity He rested, knowing His work had been accomplished. (4) *How distinguished*! He sat at God's right hand. Few people ever reach such heights of exaltation. Our High Priest is enthroned in the heavens, far above principalities and powers. (5) *How discerning*! He knew the end would never be in doubt. The battle and its issues had been won and settled at the cross of Calvary. It is thrilling to contemplate that *this Man* is our Lord and Savior. We are safe in His keeping.

THE FIFTH HIGHWAY THROUGH HEBREWS
... by the blood of Jesus

This epistle was written to Jews, and therefore it is no cause for amazement that the author had much to say about the blood of sacrifice. All Jews knew of the importance of this; it was part of daily routine. The entire nation knew that "without shedding of blood is no remission" (Heb. 9:22). Christians were taught that the blood of animals never abolished sin; it merely provided a temporary covering. The precious blood of Jesus removed it eternally. It should be remembered that *the blood* meant *the life* , for life was in the blood. (See Lev. 17:14.) When the Bible speaks of the shed blood of Christ, it means *His sinless life outpoured on the cross of Calvary.* The New Testament has much to say about this tremendous theme.

Christ entered into the holiest by his blood (Heb. 9:12)

Obviously this refers to the fact that, on the Day of Atonement, the high priest of Israel entered within the veil of temple to appear before God on behalf of the nation. (See Leviticus 16.) Engraved upon his breastplate were the names of the twelve tribes. When he stood before the mercy seat, he carried those names, not only on his heart, but also in his supplication. This was the foundation upon which priestly intercession rested. This epistle explains that, although the earthly temple no longer existed, Jesus had entered the *real temple of God*, the heavens themselves. No other man was ever permitted to proceed beyond the veil of the temple; no other person could ever approach so close to God. Christians have a unique High Priest who pleads their cause continually.

The blood of Jesus purges our conscience (Heb. 9:14)

"How much more shall the blood of Christ, who through the eternal Spirit offered himself without spot to God, *purge your conscience* from dead works to serve the living God." Christ made the atonement, the Holy Spirit applied it, and God accepted it. This had never been accomplished previously. To absolve a conscience from guilt was beyond the powers of man. The blood of a turtledove might satisfy the demands of law, but it could never bring rest to a guilty conscience. This was the forerunner of real peace; the assurance that what Christ began He would complete.

By His blood we enter the holiest of all (Heb. 10:19)

What once was a private footpath used once a year by one privileged man had become an open highway. As a marvelous and thrilling contrast to what was, there existed a new and living way by which believers could draw near to the mercy seat. We are not only able to enter and stand there; we stand there *with Him*, for He has become our advocate, our lawyer pleading a case before the Judge of all mankind. The writer to the Hebrews was able to say: "Let us draw near with a true heart in full assurance of faith, having our hearts sprinkled from an evil conscience, and our bodies washed with pure water" (v. 22). Thank God, the separating veil has been destroyed.

By His blood He sanctifies us (Heb. 13:12)

"Wherefore Jesus also, that he might sanctify the people with his own blood, suffered without the gate." Formerly, in order to sanctify any person or thing, the priest sprinkled people, and even today it is possible to witness the procedure when priests walk among crowds, spraying incense over expectant congregations. Jesus never did this kind of thing. However, the writer of this letter affirms that the merits of the work done at Calvary became a sanctifying influence spread by Christ over all who looked expectantly to Him. His precious blood not only cleansed their sins and opened a new and living way into the presence of God, it also made people acceptable before the Lord. This was the climax of all His endeavor. John 14:3 informs us that where He is, there shall we be also. Since nothing that defiles can ever enter into the presence of the living God, we need to possess something greater than the forgiveness of sin. We must be sanctified; we must reach higher ground and be conformed to the image of God's Son. 1 John 1:7 informs us that, when we walk in the light as He is in the light, the *blood of Jesus goes on cleansing us from all sin.* This process will continue until we are like Jesus. (See 1 John 3:2.) Obviously, without the assistance of Christ and the Comforter whom the Lord sent to help us, these exalted standards would be beyond our reach.

THE SIXTH HIGHWAY THROUGH HEBREWS
. . . at the right hand of God

To sit at the side of a king, queen, or president is a very great honor; and few of the inhabitants of earth ever attain to that place of exaltation. It is of interest to learn that throughout this epistle, the writer continues to emphasize the fact that Christ is seated at the right hand of the Majesty on high. The greatest honor that God could bestow was conferred upon the Savior. This indicated acceptance and approval of what He had accomplished. The work that God gave Him to do had been completed; the job was done. When God crowned Christ with glory and honor, the coronation in heaven superceded anything ever known among angels or humans.

His rightful place (Heb. 1:13)

"But to which of the angels said he at any time, Sit on my right hand, until I make thine enemies thy footstool?" Jesus had accomplished what angels could not even attempt; He had by Himself purged our sins. Christ belonged at God's right hand for two reasons. He had been there from the beginning; the place of honor was His by natural affinity with the Father. Yet, an additional reason was now evident. Having done what God desired, the Lord by right of conquest and fulfillment had *earned* His place of honor. He had reached the place of supreme exaltation by performing on earth what had been planned in heaven. Therefore, there was nothing surprising in His being at God's right hand; He was where He belonged.

His royal place (Heb. 8:1)

Apart from the mysterious Melchizedek there had never been a royal priest. A king was a king, and a priest was a priest. No man had ever filled the two positions. Royalty expressed majesty and power; the priesthood expressed concern for those represented. This picture of Christ surpassed all expectation. Seated in the heavens, our Royal Priest not only intercedes; His position suggests He is able to do what needs to be done. He resembles an ambassador. His one hand grasps the heart of God, and the other reaches down to the impoverished people of earth. He is at one and the same moment God and Man, our intercessor in another world. The realization of this eternal truth is the harbinger of peace. This was probably the reason why the great prototype Melchizedek was called both the *King of Righteousness* and the *King of Salem* — Peace.

His redemptive place (Heb. 10:12)

"But this man, after he had offered one sacrifice for sins for ever, *sat down on the right hand of God.*" Read John 20:17 and consider how, on the first Easter morning, the Lord made a visit to heaven. Doubtless He went to present His credentials, for no priest could represent Israel until he himself had been accepted by God. Never throughout the gospels was Christ revealed as the High Priest of His people. According to the law, a priest could only exercise his ministry after the sacrifice had been made. Calvary changed the Lord. He had become more than a friend or teacher. He was planning to do for His people more than had ever been done. The reconciliation made through His death made it possible for Him to sit on a real *throne of grace.* The ancient priests sprinkled the blood of sacrifice on and before the mercy seat. Many theologians believe that Christ went home to heaven to present His blood as the credential by which He could be installed as the High Priest of believers. When God accepted that credential the Lord was crowned with glory and honor, and from that hallowed moment Jesus became our representative in the greatest court in the universe.

His radiant place (Heb. 12:2)

"Looking unto Jesus the author and finisher of our faith; who for the joy that was set before him endured the cross, despising the shame, and *is set down at the right hand of the throne of God.*" Jesus never tried to avoid what men considered to be the ultimate tragedy. Each time He thought of the cross, He was thrilled with joyful expectancy, realizing it was the appointed way by which many sons would be brought to glory. We also must shun anything that might hinder progress toward the eternal home. Christ was present when our Christian experience began; He will be there at journey's end. Therefore "let us run with patience the race that is set before us, *looking unto Jesus.*" The path of life may be difficult, it may run through shadowy territory, but Christians should know "the path of the just" leads to the "perfect day" (Prov. 4:18).

THE SEVENTH HIGHWAY THROUGH HEBREWS . . . the end of all the roads

The age in which the letter to the Hebrews was written was a period of uncertainty. Old religious regimes had terminated; people hardly knew what to expect next. Many Christians were becoming martyrs, the ferocity unleashed against them was frightening, and every man and woman wondered if he or she would be the next victim. The outlook was exceedingly bleak and, for many joy had become elusive. Many students believe Paul was the author of this letter, but the identity of the writer is not of supreme importance. In the midst of uncertainty, God stressed the certainties of life and by so doing summed up what had been said throughout the epistle. Here we have the gospel in a nutshell!

Our problem is acute (Heb. 9:27).

"It is appointed unto men once to die." This fact is unassailable. No person can deny that the end of mortality is death. The wealthy and the poor, the educated and the illiterate, adults and children, the people of all creeds and color will reach the end of their earthly journey. Accumulated possessions will be left behind; friends and family, at best, can only attend our funerals. It must always be a cause for regret that even the wisest of human beings have never been able to discover a way to avoid or defeat this archenemy of mankind. It is appointed — that is, it has been ordained — that humans cannot live on earth forever. That is the human races greatest problem.

Our predicament is alarming (Heb. 9:27).

"But after [death] the judgment." This is probably considered by many people to be the most unpleasant message in the Scriptures. All kinds of teachers have tried to minimize the somber fact that men are accountable to God. The idea that the Almighty could ever punish offenders is considered by liberal teachers to be obnoxious. Everybody likes to think of heaven with its glories, but the contemplation of a day of judgment is unwanted and unpleasant. Men like to believe that the grace of God will always be greater than human guilt; hence there is never need to worry. However pleasant and desirable that interpretation may be, the fact remains that it is not in accordance with the words spoken by Jesus. He warned people about a day of reckoning and said that, if they died unforgiven, they would be lost eternally. This terrible reality should fill men with dread.

Our pardon is achievable (Heb. 9:28).

"So Christ was once offered to bear the sins of many." The entire epistle explains that Christ, the Lamb of God, fulfilled the types and shadows found in the Old Testament and that He took our sins and nailed them, so to speak, to the cross of Calvary. In the merit of His precious blood, He satisfied the requirements of divine law and, having sacrificed Himself for our sin, sat down at the right hand of the throne of God. There He intercedes for His people and dispenses forgiveness to those who seek it. There is no need to fear the day of judgment. If our sins are pardoned, no charge can be made against us. Our High Priest can testify to the fact that, because He paid our debt, we are free from condemnation. Confidence in this truth removes dread. "He that heareth my word, and believeth on him that sent me, hath everlasting life, *and shall not come into condemnation;* but is passed from death unto life" (John 5:24).

Our promise is assured (Heb. 9:28).

"And unto them that look for him shall he appear the second time without sin unto salvation." This is the greatest of all the certainties mentioned in this epistle. The Lord Jesus Christ is seated at the right hand of the throne of God, but His position there is only temporary. He promised to return to this world. God said that Jesus should inherit the throne of His father David; therefore, when Christ reigns for a thousand years, the seat of His kingdom will be in Jerusalem. There is reason to believe that the promise of His return is the brightest star in God's prophetical sky. Evil may appear to win occasional battles, but the final triumph rests with God. "Jesus shall reign wher-e'er the sun does his successive journeys run, His kingdom spread from shore to shore till moons shall wax and wane no more."

It is easy to understand why the writer of this letter urged his readers to look "unto Jesus." When despondency and fear threaten the tranquility of the soul, when approaching peril chills the human spirit, the best and safest way to avoid trouble is to look "unto Jesus" (Heb. 12:2). It is better to look for a sunrise than to close one's eyes and remain in the dark!

JOHN . . . who believed that Christians should be Christlike! (1 John 2:6)

John was the last of the apostles to rejoin the Lord in heaven. He lived to be over ninety years of age and during his lifetime saw many changes within the church. When he reminisced, he remembered the years when he walked and talked with Christ; he remembered the period when the church was weak, yet tremendously powerful. Alas, the egotism of certain leaders had damaged the assemblies. Diotrephes had assumed illegal authority and had denied fellowship to some of God's greatest servants. It was this unpleasant fact that led John to issue his most trenchant statement. He said, "He that saith he abideth in [Christ] ought himself also so to walk, even as he walked."

A soul promised

This text is a diamond with many facets, each of which reflects eternal truth. *The New English Bible* translates the text as follows: "He who claims to be in Christ, *binds himself* to live as He lived." Behind this statement is the thought of betrothal. Marriage in the Middle East was not what it has become in Western countries. A girl was promised to a suitor even in the earliest days of infancy; the marriage was arranged by the father; and, although the vows could not be consummated until years later, the contract was made early in the young girl's life. To enter into marriage inferred that the bride was not only to embrace her husband, but also to enter into, and participate in, the life he lived. When she married a fisherman, she consented to share the life of a fisherman. If she married a business man, she promised to share his type of life, to help him in all his activities,to share both his success and failure. John insisted that any person who voluntarily undertook to become part of the bride of Christ automatically confessed willingness to live the same type of life He lived. Anything short of that was a violation of matrimony.

A soul possessed

J. B. Phillips provides a translation reflecting another facet of this important verse. "He who professes to be living in God, must bear *the stamp of Christ.*" Betrothal indicated a promise had been made. Ownership suggested the marriage had taken place; the bride belonged to her husband. The ring on her finger indicated ownership. This truth was also expressed in the life of a bond slave. A slave who had learned to love his master was given the opportunity to remain in his service forever. When this decision was made, the ear of the man was pierced, and this became the sign of ownership.

He voluntarily became the property of his beloved Master. It was impossible for a slave to belong to two masters — he belonged to one only. Canadian trees are felled by many logging companies, but each tree carries the stamp of ownership. Thousands of logs float down the rivers to the gathering place where the trees are separated for use in various mills. Once the mark is on the log, its identity is never confused. John insisted that this type of ownership should be evident in the conduct of every believer. Christians belong to Christ and no one else. Any conduct unbecoming of Christ would be a disgrace. We should walk as He walked.

A soul privileged

Vincent, in *The Amplified New Testament,* expresses another thought. The word translated "ought" is *opheilie*, which means "to owe a debt"! Hence the translation "He who claims to abide in Him, ought *as a personal debt*, to conduct himself as Christ did." This becomes obvious when we consider the parable of the vine. (See John 15:4-5.) A branch could not exist apart from the vine; therefore, it becomes the duty of the branch to pay its debt of gratitude by producing the kind of fruit desired by the vine. John insisted that Christians owe their existence to the Savior.

All we have, are, and hope to be is centered in the Lord Jesus. His love sought us; His blood bought us; His grace brought us into the fold: His unending patience has tolerated our inconsistencies since the first day we met Him. Therefore it is incumbent we do everything possible to repay at least some of the immense debt owed to Him. Nevertheless, this should never be considered a duty. It should always be life's greatest privilege to serve the Lord who bought us with His precious blood. When John uttered this tremendous statement, he was thinking of the arrogant leader who had become a dictator, whose biased ideas dominated the church, and whose dictates prevented brethren from enjoying fellowship. In actual fact the Lord's Table had been sealed off by a fence constructed by the warped ideas of Diotrephes. Obviously his being *in the church* was not a guarantee *he was in Christ.*

THE CHURCH AT EPHESUS . . . and waning enthusiasm

(REVELATION 2:4)

The letters sent to the seven churches of Asia have always been interesting because of the possibility of a two-fold interpretation of their content. Some theological teachers insist the messages were only of local importance; that is, John was writing to individual churches and had no intention his words should be used out of context. Others, equally emphatic, believed the churches were "chosen" to be representative of seven phases of church history, events from Pentecost until the removal of the church to heaven. It does not matter, for the purposes of this study, which of the two viewpoints is acceptable. The message concerning overcoming relates to Christians in every age.

A fervent commencement

It should always be remembered that, when Paul went to Ephesus, the city was entirely idolatrous. The goddess Diana touched every section of city life and prevailed throughout Asia. Luke describes how Paul, at the risk of his life, boldly challenged the power of heathenism and established what was probably the most famous of the New Testament churches. The letter which the apostle sent to the Ephesians eloquently testifies to the quality of the members and the depth of their theological understanding. Within the scope of six chapters, the writer explained the deeper teachings of the Christian life and encompassed eternity. (See Eph. 1:4; 5:27.) The Ephesian assembly was probably the greatest Bible-loving church in existence at that time, and John admitted that feature had remained unchanged. Liberal interpretations of divine truth were not tolerated among the members, and people who did not believe the fundamentals of the faith never occupied their pulpit.

A famous church

The Christians in Ephesus set a standard of truth for all believers, and the words found in Revelation 2:1-3 indicate the careful methods used in ascertaining the worth of every preacher. "Thou hast tried them which say they are apostles, and are not, and hast found them liars." It is significant that when Paul made his last journey to Jerusalem, the elders of the church met him at Miletus and wept with their friend. At that point in time, the church had not declined, although Paul warned them of approaching perils. (See Acts 20:29.) After some years the situation had changed dramatically. The church was still fundamentally strong, but the initial enthusiasm was beginning to wane. Their "first love" for Christ had somewhat diminished. This was certainly a description of the church at the end of the first century.

A frightening concern

"Nevertheless I have somewhat against thee, because thou hast left thy first love. Remember therefore from whence thou hast fallen, and repent, and do the first works; or else I will come unto thee quickly, and will remove thy candlestick [lampstand] out of his place, except thou repent" (Rev. 2:4-5). Unfortunately, what happened in Ephesus was characteristic of all the churches. They remained sound in doctrine, but their early enthusiasm for the cause of Christ waned. The result was devastating. The passionate zeal for the extension of the kingdom of Christ began to disappear. As a result, if it had not been for the arrival of the apostle Paul, the world outreach of evangelism would have been seriously hindered.

A fabulous challenge

Their dying enthusiasm became the greatest concern of the Lord, and the message sent through John reminded the assembly they were in danger of losing most of what they had gained. When the Lord spoke of overcoming, He obviously referred to their complacency. They needed to stir themselves and face the future with a determination to succeed. The Savior promised that they who did as He requested would be permitted "to eat of the tree of life, which is in the midst of the paradise of God" (v. 7). It is worthy of consideration that this tree may be found at the beginning and end of the Bible. (See Gen. 2:9; 3:22 and Rev. 22:2.) The tree in both instances was the means by which God could impart eternal life to obedient people. Adam might have become a partaker of the divine nature, but alas, he sinned and died. Through the grace of God the same privilege was afforded to believers in Christ. 2 Peter 1:4 reminds us that we may be "partakers of the divine nature." Finally, at the end of time, the Jews and other earth dwellers will also have that identical opportunity when "the last enemy that shall be destroyed is death" (1 Cor. 15:24-26). The chance to partake of the fullness of the life of God is an inestimable privilege, the greatness of which will never be fully known until we stand in His presence. Overcoming has never been easy in anything, but the reward offered in these verses is so great that Christians cannot afford to be apathetic.

THE CHURCH AT SMYRNA . . . and weakening endurance (REVELATION 2:9-10)

The seven churches of Asia to which John sent his letters had three things in common: (1) *Overwhelming problems;* (2) *Overwrought people;* and (3) *Overcoming promises.* These were very evident in the message sent to the Christians in Smyrna. To understand the implications of this letter, it is necessary to know the historical background of the city. Strategically, Smyrna was a formidable bridgehead between the East and West; and magistrates, recognizing the importance of an alliance with Rome, had arranged a treaty of mutual assistance. They had dispatched ships to assist their allies, and as a reward were given permission to erect a temple to the deity of the emperor. It also contained a very hostile synagogue that persecuted Christians, and in A.D. 155 Bishop Polycarp became a martyr for the cause of Christ. It was very difficult to be a Christian in Smyrna, for many enemies were informers. Persecution led to much sorrow. This letter sent by John acknowledged the problems and explained overcoming was their greatest need.

Overcoming persecution and distress

"Fear none of those things which thou shalt suffer; behold, the devil shall cast some of you into prison, that ye may be tried; and ye shall have tribulation ten days . . . " (v. 10). This may be a reference to the fact that there were ten periods of persecution to be endured by the early church, and that the final one lasted exactly ten years. Persecution continued until A.D. 311, but conditions improved when Constantine, the Emperor, exhibited interest in the Christian faith and embraced the new doctrine. The fear of death became a menace to some of the younger believers, and therefore John thought it necessary to encourage them to endure. The anticipation of receiving a crown of life was meant to help the fearful to remain faithful, but it was not easy to do this when authorities were seeking an excuse to torture believers in Jesus. John contrasted two kinds of death. The first indicated the end of physical existence in this world; it destroyed the body. The second referred to the tragedy that destroyed both body and soul in eternity. (See Rev. 20:14.)

Overcoming persistence unto death

It is not known how many of the Smyrna Christians laid down their lives for the Savior, nor is it known how many faltered before continuing attrocities. When heads were severed from bodies and believers were set alight to amuse heathens, it became increasingly difficult for members of the church to remain true to Christ. History attests the fact they were required to burn incense before the great altar erected in honor of Caesar; it also tells how people who refused to do so were accused of treason and tortured until they recanted or died. It is easy for people who live unmolested to criticize their ancient brethren, but perhaps the indifference of modern Christians deserves greater condemnation than the weakening faith of others who were literally skinned alive. It would seem that the prophetical theologians have reason to believe that this message to Smyrna was a true indication of the sufferings of Christians to be endured during the first centuries of the history of the church.

Overcoming and protection

"He that overcometh shall not be hurt of the second death" (v. 11). This appears to be the other side of the picture presented in the letter to the Ephesians. The first church was reminded of the inestimable privilege of sharing in the fullness of the life of God. This church was promised they would never lose what they had gained. The term "the second death" refers to the calamity when sinners are rejected at the throne of God's justice. Banished eternally from the presence of the Almighty, the guilty are sent to a place of unending sorrow. This is known as the second death; it is an experience which knows no remorse, no hope, no Savior, and no end. Overcomers need not fear this tragedy. When God forgave their sins, He also forgot them; they will never be remembered again. (See Jer. 31:34.) Jesus also said, "Verily, verily, I say unto you, He that heareth my word, and believeth on him that sent me, hath everlasting life, *and shall not come into condemnation;* but is passed from death unto life" (John 5:24). The saints at Smyrna had great need to consider the words of Paul who wrote, "For I reckon that the sufferings of this present time are not worthy to be compared with the glory which shall be revealed in us" (Rom. 8:18). *Weak believers* may face their problems and then ask, "What will it cost *if I do* my duty and remain true to Christ? *Wise believers* ask a different question: "How much will it cost *if I do not* remain true to Christ?" When Lot chose the plains of Sodom, he embarked on a journey that ruined him. When Abraham climbed into the everlasting hills, he was not only assured of excellent company, but also laying up "treasures in heaven, where neither moth nor rust doth corrupt, and where thieves do not break through nor steal" (Matt. 6:20). It is healthier to breathe pure air in the mountain than to be choked by smog in a valley.

THE CHURCH AT PERGAMOS . . . and wavering endeavor

(REVELATION 2:14-17)

Pergamos was one of the most idolatrous cities in the ancient world, for within its precincts three religious cults had their headquarters. On a cliff overlooking the city was an altar to the god Zeus, and throughout the city were many shrines dedicated either to Athena, the virgin goddess of wisdom, war, arts, and crafts, or to the deity of the emperor of Rome. All these movements were hostile to the Christian church.

An iniquitous city

It is significant that John wrote: "I know thy works, and where thou dwellest, *even where Satan's seat is:* and thou holdest fast my name, and hast not denied my faith, even in those days wherein Antipas was my faithful martyr, who was slain among you, *where Satan dwelleth*" (Rev. 2:13). The apostle's statement indicates the ferocity of the attacks made against the members of the Christian church. We do not know how many people sacrificed their lives for Christ in the city, but tradition says Antipas was the first to suffer martyrdom because of his refusal to obey the commands of the authorities. Tradition says he was incinerated inside a brazen bull. The ancient writer Pausanias, writing about Pergamos, "described the throne-like altar to Zeus on the top of the crag above the city. It was discovered in 1871 and taken to Germany, where it stands reconstructed today in the East Berlin Museum." (Quoted from *The Zondervan Pictorial Encyclopedia of the Bible.* Volume 4; p. 702.) Rome frowned upon any movement that threatened the sovereignty and unity of the empire, and thus it was no cause for amazement when the officials tried to silence the preachers of Pergamos. When Christians refused to burn incense before the pagan gods, they were tortured. Many of the monuments discovered by archaeologists give mute testimony to the ruthlessness of the heathen persecutors.

An insidious compromise

A new type of problem confronted the Christians of Pergamos; it was the temptation to compromise. There were great differences of opinion between the heathen systems, but when the church opposed any one of the three, at least two of the rival religions supported their assertions. This fact led to compromise. Many thought it would be better to cooperate and live than resist and die. They reasoned it would be wiser to give a little, if they could gain much. Therefore, when they were requested to burn incense, some of them did so and then tried to ignore the fact their testimony had been undermined. John condemned this procedure and reminded his readers of the strange prophet Balaam whose actions were denounced by his donkey. (See Num. 22-25.) John insisted that believers in Christ should never compromise with a system that had crucified the Lord. A man was either in the kingdom or not; it was unwise to stand with one foot in the kingdom of Christ and the other in a place where idolatry was rampant. If John were writing to modern Christians, he would emphasize the same truth.

An inspired challenge

It would appear that one of the smaller sects was known as Nicolaitans, whose influence had contaminated the assembly. The name was derived from two words. Niko meant "to conquer," and laos meant "the people or laity." A group of laymen had arisen to claim that a little compromise was necessary to save the church from extinction. Nevertheless, the church, although living, was beginning to die. The rewards of overcoming as expressed by the Lord were singularly attractive. The Savior promised that they who overcame this very seductive problem would be rewarded two-fold. First, they would be permitted to eat of the hidden manna. That promise may have been related to the message given by Jesus in John 6:48-50, or it may refer to the God-given manna preserved in the ark of the covenant. Victorious saints would enjoy pleasures unknown to those who did not triumph in the battles of life.

The mention of "a white stone" related to an ancient custom among travelers. When a guest left a home, he gave to his host one-half of a white stone. Then he would say, "When I came to you, I received a welcome. Some day you might come to my country, and if you do, bring that stone with you. It will remind me of your kindness. It will then be my pleasure to do for you in my land, what you did for me in yours." Every member of the Pergamos church was aware of that custom and would have appreciated the significance of John's words. The Savior had left His own land to visit earth. His hand had knocked on the door of the hearts of the people, many of whom had invited Him to enter. (See Rev. 3:20.) They knew they would eventually visit the Lord's country and could expect a similar welcome to that already given on earth. This was one of the most wonderful promises ever given by Christ to His followers. It not only represented a reward for overcoming; it described a privilege too great to be sacrificed on an altar of compromise.

Margin Ref for 2 V 17 (whitestone)
Chapter 3 - V 12. To Him that overcometh etc
Revelations-

THE CHURCH AT THYATIRA . . . and wicked enticement

(REVELATION 2:25-28)

The letter written by John to the church at Thyatira was probably the most intriguing of all the messages sent to the Christians in Asia. This was because he mentioned a mysterious woman named Jezebel. "Thou sufferest that woman Jezebel, which calleth herself a prophetess, to teach and to seduce my servants" (2:20). Very little is known of this person except that some teachers believe she was a leader among the Nicolaitans or a high official in one of the many guilds based in the city. "Inscriptions are not numerous, but they mention workers in wool, linen, leather, and bronze, potters, bakers, dyers, and slavers. Each had their guild like that of the silversmiths of Ephesus." (*The Zondervan Pictorial Encyclopedia of the Bible.* Volume 5, p. 743.) However, it is difficult to believe "a prophetess" could teach in a church if she were a leader in a heathen organization.

The prophetical significance

It is worthy of attention that all seven of the churches who received a letter from John were for the most part in close proximity to Ephesus, where Paul ministered for two years. They were probably begun by the apostle, and therefore it is difficult to understand why they were so different. The church at Ephesus lost its first love; the Christians at Smyrna struggled against persecution; the assembly in Pergamos was told not to compromise; the believers in Thyatira were rebuked for permitting the ministry of a false prophetess. These details present problems — unless the assemblies were *chosen* to represent different periods in church history.

It can hardly be coincidental that the word pictures given by John should match later events. At the end of the first century, the zeal of the early church had almost vanished. Then, for almost three centuries, fierce persecution devastated the churches, and many saints laid down their lives for Christ. The third period began with the conversion of the Emperor Constantine, after which all kinds of worldly temptations confronted believers. After these events the Roman Church became dominant, enforcing her authority with torture and death. This might have been the fulfillment of the prophetical significance of the Jezebel mentioned in the letter to Thyatira. Things were done in the name of Christ that were infinitely removed from the pattern given in the New Testament. Priests burned Christians to death, and things were taught which, if judged by the Scriptures, could only be called blasphemous. These unfortunate events produced the Reformation, when Martin Luther nailed his thesis to the door of his church in Wittenberg, Germany.

The powerful statement

"But that which ye have already hold fast till I come. And he that overcometh, and keepeth my works unto the end, to him will I give power over the nations: And he shall rule them with a rod of iron" (2:25-26). The promise of eminence within the kingdom of Christ was conditional upon "keeping my works *unto the end.*" Entrance into the kingdom was assured the moment a person was accepted into the family of God; *his position* within the kingdom will be finalized at the judgment seat of Christ. (See 1 Cor. 3:13-15.) It behooves all followers of Christ to be faithful unto death; otherwise they might lose their crowns. (See Rev. 3:11.) The sequence of thought here is challenging. If Jezebel succeeded in poisoning the soul with false teachings, the Christian inevitably suffered. Apathy replaced zeal, and disaster followed. Paul was wise when he reminded the Ephesian church that "We wrestle not against flesh and blood, but against principalities, against powers, against the rulers of the darkness of this world, against spiritual wickedness in high places" (Eph. 6:12). There was need to overcome at all times.

The promised star

"And I will give him the morning star." It is wise to remember the Lord said, "I am the root and the offspring of David, and the bright and morning star" (Rev. 22:16). The morning star is the harbinger of dawn, the evidence that night is ending and that sunrise is near. When we connect this statement with the command, "hold fast till I come," the significance becomes clear. The return of the Savior will be as a star in the heavens, evidence that earth's night will be terminating and that heaven's day is at hand. Then, the Lord will give Himself to those who overcame in the struggles of life so that they might be together eternally. What this means we may never know until it happens. The morning star is one of the most attractive sights in the firmament. That overcomers will be just as beautiful is assured, for John said, "We know that, when he shall appear, we shall be like him; for we shall see him as he is" (1 John 3:2).

THE CHURCH AT SARDIS . . . and woeful emptiness

(REVELATION 3:1)

Sardis was the capital city of a flourishing territory; it stood on a hill fifteen hundred feet above a very fertile plain. The place became famous under the reign of Croesus, and it was there that gold and silver coins first appeared. The city was considered to be impregnable, and this produced an apathy that led to its downfall. One episode of its history was described by the historian Herodotus who wrote: "On the fourteenth day of the seige, Cyrus made proclamation that he would give a reward to the man who should first mount the wall. . . . One Hyroeades resolved to approach the citadel and attempt it at a place where no guards were ever set. On this side the rock was so precipitous, and the citadel so impregnable, that no fear was entertained of its being taken in this place. . . . Hyroeades, however, had observed a Lydian soldier descend the rock to retrieve a helmet which had rolled down from the top, and having seen the man pick it up and carry it back, thought over what he had witnessed, and formed his plan. He climbed the rock himself, and other Persians followed in his track until a large number was mounted to the top. Thus Sardis was taken." Complacency based on a false sense of security led to the downfall of the stronghold. It was nothing short of a miracle that the Christian church was established in this formidable place, but the Christians became like the people among whom they lived.

An empty profession

"Thou hast a name that thou livest, and art dead" (3:1). Emphasis had been placed on formalism; the church members said all the right words and performed the correct acts but had no passion for the cause of Christ. It was said of some that, because they had not defiled their garments, they would walk with Christ in white because they were worthy. The Lord said of others that they had need to repent and "strengthen the things which remain; that are ready to die." When a Christian becomes completely content with his service for Christ, he has reached the end of his usefulness. Religion can be very disappointing. A form of godliness without the power of God can be as damning as unbelief. The gospel reminds readers that Nicodemus and the Pharisees were religious and practiced its precepts. Other religions around the world have their man-made laws, but Christianity produces love which knows no limits in serving the risen Lord. Dead dogma is an idea affecting the human mind; the power of the Holy Spirit transforms a life. Unless this quality be manifested among believers, their church is only a building in which meetings are held.

An enormous possibility

"Remember therefore how thou hast received and heard, and hold fast, and repent. If therefore thou shalt not watch, I will come on thee as a thief, and thou shalt not know what hour I will come upon thee." Here there may be a veiled reference to the incident when a Syrian soldier climbed the cliff to take the city. A church may be theologically sound and yet its spiritual life be in danger. As Tarsus fell, so the church could disintegrate and become a memory. John reminded the believers that there was need to repent, for precious things were dying. It seems strange that once again the prophetical interpretation of these letters appears to be vindicated. When Luther rebelled against the Jezebel of the Middle Ages, the reformation spread across Europe. The reformers enjoyed an enviable reputation, but discord ruined their work. Men who rejected ecclesiastical authority became a law unto themselves and were convinced they alone correctly interpreted the Scriptures. When they argued among themselves, the new church almost perished.

An entrancing promise

"He that overcometh, the same shall be clothed in white raiment; and I will not blot out his name out of the book of life, but I will confess his name before my Father, and before his angels" (3:5). The reward promised to overcomers was threefold. (1) "The same shall be clothed in white raiment." The fine linen represents the righteousness of the saints (see Rev. 19:8) and is related to those to be invited to the marriage of the Lamb, the greatest event ever to happen. (2) "I will not blot out his name out of the book of life." The book of life is mentioned frequently throughout the Bible, but other books are also mentioned. (See Rev. 20:12-15.) While we remain on earth, we may not completely understand these words, but obviously it is possible to enjoy eternal security in Christ. (3) "I will confess his name before my Father, and before his angels." Could there be any greater joy than hearing one's name on the lips of the Son of God? Could there be any greater satisfaction than to hear Him say, "Well done, thou good and faithful servant, enter thou into the joy of thy Lord"? The best is yet to be — if we become overcomers.

THE CHURCH AT PHILADELPHIA . . . and wonderful ecstasy

(REVELATION 3:8)

The churches at Smyrna and Philadelphia were the only two of the seven assemblies in Asia that appeared to be blameless in the Lord's estimation. The first endured through times of terrible persecution; the second was presented with the challenge of an open door. These teach: (1) However heavy burdens may be, they could be heavier. (2) However good a church may be, there is still room for improvement. The former preserves confidence; the latter promotes humility. The message sent to Philadelphia divides into four sections.

The challenge of an open door

"Behold, I have set before thee an open door, and no man can shut it." The greatest danger confronting a successful church is contemplative satisfaction. The members look back at accomplishments and around at achievements and then exclaim, "We have done it!" Any pastor who is completely satisfied with his work should resign and do God a favor! It is wise to reminisce and be grateful; it is wonderful to look around and rejoice. But it is infinitely better to look ahead and determine to do better. There are times when ecstasy contributes to pride; it is wiser and safer to remember that we might have done even more had we tried harder. The church of brotherly love had performed miracles in Christ's name, but believing the members could reach higher levels of accomplishment. The Lord set before them an open door, which no man could close.

The certainty of an outstanding deliverance

"Because thou hast kept the word of my patience, *I also will keep thee from the hour of temptation,* which shall come upon all the world, *to try them that dwell upon the earth*" (v. 10). This verse is very difficult to explain unless the prophetical interpretation of the seven letters be correct. It is almost impossible to comprehend how any local church could be delivered from a catastrophe reaching the entire planet. There has never been an international tragedy of such dimensions. It has been claimed this church represents the sixth period of church history, a time reaching from A.D. 1750 until A.D. 1900, when the church made special efforts to help a sinful world. It was then that missionary enterprise gained a new momentum, pioneer missionaries went to the unreached parts of the earth, and a new era of evangelical activity commenced. Similarly, it has been claimed the Laodicean church exhibited characteristics to be evident immediately before the homegoing of the saints. (See 1 Thess. 4:16-18.) The Bible teaches that, after the rapture of the church, the Antichrist will dominate the earth, and unprecedented times of anguish will overwhelm its inhabitants. This will reach *the whole earth,* and therefore it would seem that a very special promise was given to those who loved and served the Lord.

The compulsion of an overcoming determination

"Behold, I come quickly: hold that fast which thou hast, that no man take thy crown" (v. 11). In spite of magnificent success, the members of the church in Philadelphia needed to hold fast; there was danger that neglect and apathy might be followed by the loss of eternal rewards. The struggle would never end until it was over! The conflict would not terminate until the final shot had been fired! Paul said, "This one thing I do, forgetting those things which are behind, and reaching forth unto those things which are before, I *press toward the mark for the prize of the high calling of God in Christ Jesus"* (Phil. 3:13-14). As athletes, the saints in Philadelphia were urged to lay aside every weight and to make a supreme effort to run their race triumphantly. (See Heb. 12:1-2.)

The celebration of overwhelming delight

The triple mention of "writing upon the believer" invites investigation. During the Lord's sojourn on earth, He only wrote on one occasion. (See John 8:6-8.) Here at the end of life's journey, He would write three things: (1) The name of my God, (2) The name of the city of my God, and (3) My new name. To write one's name on an article is to assert ownership; a name on a painting indicates the artist is not ashamed of his work. To write a name on a check or bequest is an indication of authority, dependability, and enablement. That Jesus should write on the saints of Philadelphia probably expressed all of these features. He was proud of His work; He had brought men and women safely to glory, and they would be exhibited throughout eternity. They were the work of His own hands! Furthermore, the name of the city of God, the New Jerusalem, indicated where they belonged; they were a very privileged class of people, the prized possession of the Prince of Heaven. All who aspire to such exaltation should pay attention to the words of Jesus. "He that hath an ear, let him hear what the Spirit saith unto the churches." No sacrifice can be too great when so much is being offered.

THE CHURCH AT LAODICEA . . . and its wealthy environment (REVELATION 3:15-18)

Laodicea was a very important post on a trade route used by the Romans in the Middle East. It stood on an elevation one hundred feet above the Lycus River but, unfortunately, was frequently damaged by earthquakes. The citizens were extremely affluent, for, in addition to the income gained from contact with foreign legions, wealth was derived from the wool of black sheep, which created a prosperous industry for the area. Laodicea was also famous for a special poultice, a medication widely used in the treatment of eye diseases. History says Antiochus the Great permitted 2,000 Jewish families to settle in the country, and doubtless that explained the presence of a strong Jewish synagogue. The gentile citizens were idolaters. An acquaintance with these details is necessary for an understanding of the Laodicean letter.

A devastating statement . . . "I will spue thee out of my mouth."

The Lord, through John, said, "I know thy works, that thou art neither cold nor hot. I would thou wert cold or hot. So then . . . I will spue thee out of my mouth." After a terrible earthquake, the citizens of Laodicea, from their own financial resources, completely rebuilt the city. The church members had become exceptionally rich, but love of money ruined their testimony. Instead of their "being in the world but not of it," worldliness dominated every aspect of religious life. It was a church that would have overflowing congregations at special events but very few at a prayer meeting. They contributed generously toward missionary activities but never became missionaries. Their building, in all probability, was a very attractive structure, but the architect never arranged to include a penitent form in his master plan. Although everything appeared to be wonderful, the spiritual life of the church was disappointing.

A deceiving situation . . . "Thou knowest not"

"Because thou sayest, I am rich, and increased with goods, and have need of nothing; and knowest not that thou art wretched, and miserable, and poor, and blind, and naked; I counsel thee to buy of me gold tried in the fire, that thou mayst be rich; and white raiment, that thou mayest be clothed, and that the shame of thy nakedness do not appear; and anoint thine eyes with eyesalve, that thou mayest see" (vv. 17-18). John's letter obviously referred to the assets of the city, the things that made Laodicea famous. Their trade produced wealth; their wool and clothing provided the finest garments; their medication for eye diseases was sought by innumerable people. Although the people gave assistance to others, their own needs remained unrecognized. They were extremely poor; their type of currency was not acceptable in heaven's bank! The beautiful clothing was transparent; it could not hide their shame. Their lotion, or poultice, restored eyesight to those going blind, but unfortunately it could not remove the cataracts from the eyes of the church members.

A divine suppliant . . . "Behold, I stand at the door and knock."

It was almost incomprehensible that the Lord should desire to enter such a church. The text suggests that if Christ were standing at the door knocking, He was not inside! To see the Lord on the outside of what professedly was His own assembly was shocking. To hear His plea asking for admittance suggested eternal love never ceased to strive with men — until there was no alternative!

This was the message sent to the last of the seven churches, and it probably represented the closing period of the church age. After the completion of the third chapter of the Revelation, the church was no longer seen on earth. The scene had changed, and attention was focused on eternity. "After this I looked, and, behold, a door was opened in heaven" (Rev. 4:1). The evangelical content of the message to Laodicea becomes obvious. Men whose trust had been in earthly treasures were asked to renounce their former ways to permit the entrance of the Savior. This promised wealth of another type; to refuse to admit the Lord was to run the risk of His leaving — forever!

A distinctive seat . . . "to sit with me."

"To him that overcometh will I grant to sit with me in my throne, even as I also overcame, and am set down with my Father in his throne" (3:21). No pew in a church could compare with a seat at the right hand of the Son of God. It is thought-provoking that every letter sent by the Lord had an identical conclusion. "He that hath an ear, let him hear what the spirit saith unto the churches." The Lord seemed to be saying, "If you have ears, use them!" A comparison of the letters sent to the people in Asia confirms that the "overcoming" part of the messages continued from Ephesus to Laodicea. Correspondingly, from the cradle to the grave, from conversion to the day we stand in the presence of our Lord, the battle will continue. Blessed is he who can say, "I can do all things through Christ which strengtheneth me" (Phil. 4:13).

CHRIST . . . and His high-rise apartments

(REVELATION 21:16)

During Bible times and for centuries afterward, high-rise apartments, or skyscrapers, as they are sometimes called, were unknown. Nomadic tribes lived in tents; and, when communities enlarged, buildings spread outward rather than upward. Vast areas of land were available, and population explosions presented no problems. Conditions have now changed dramatically. In many parts of the world, land has become very expensive. To meet the ever increasing needs of industry, high-rise buildings appear to be the only economical way to solve the problem of expansion. It is therefore thought-provoking to discover that high-rise buildings were not originally a discovery nor a solution created by men. The Bible describes a city fifteen hundred miles high!

Abraham sought a city (Heb. 11:8-10)

When the patriarch left his home in Ur of the Chaldees, he went on his journey, not knowing what his destination would be; he went in response to God's call; he went in faith, relying on the promises of the Almighty. Centuries later, the writer of the Epistle to the Hebrews said, "Abraham . . . looked for a city which hath foundations, whose builder and maker is God." It is not easy to interpret that statement. There is no evidence to prove that he looked for a city already in existence; neither is there anything to prove that he looked for God's city to be known as Jerusalem. That city was built by its original inhabitants — the Jebusites. Abraham the Seer, who saw Christ's day, was surely looking for an eternal residence — the home of the living God.

Christ promised a city (John 14:1-3)

Jesus said to His disciples, "I go to prepare a place for you." Obviously the Lord intended to erect an eternal home for His people, and the joyful anticipation of that glorious destination was meant to banish any fears harassing the disciples. How the erection was begun, continued, and completed we may not understand until we get there. God originally made the world out of nothing and designed every piece of artistry to enhance the wonder of His creation. There is reason to expect even greater beauty in the many mansions of the eternal city. Its scintillating beauty will surpass excellence and beg description.

John described the city (Rev. 21:16)

The facts and measurements of the city to come down from God out of heaven are astonishing. The details supplied by John were recently fed into a computer, and the results were beyond comprehension. The original author of the following paragraph remains unknown, but the details were copied from one of America's best known magazines.

"The city itself is said to be 12,000 furlongs (1,500 miles) square. If it descended upon the earth, it would cover two-thirds of the United States of America. Its walls would be 260 feet across, the length of a city block. They would contain 401,850 cubic feet of pure jasper. If the city were laid out in blocks 500 feet square, with the streets 100 feet wide, there would be 15,840 blocks in each side of the city. If each residence were 100 by 200 feet wide, or 20,000 square feet, there would be 12 residences in each block. This would total 3 billion, 10 million, 867,000 on the ground floor alone. Allowing twenty feet for each floor, the city would be 396,000 floors high. Assuming there would be six to ten inhabitants in each residence, we would have as neighbors, 11 quadrillion, 923 trillion, 34 billion, 112 million inhabitants. This would be if the city were in the shape of a cube." If, as I believe, the New Jerusalem will be in the shape of a pyramid, the number of inhabitants would be correspondingly fewer, but there would still be room to accommodate 1 million times the entire population that has ever lived on the earth." (Copied from the author's book: *What in the World Will Happen Next?*, pp. 175-176. Original author unknown.)

Many references supplied by the Bible lead us to believe that God is now preparing an eternal home for His redeemed people; it will exceed anything ever known by man. The details supplied by John in the last book of the Scriptures excite the soul. "The throne of God and the Lamb shall be in it; and his servants shall serve him: And they shall see his face; and his name shall be in their foreheads. And there shall be no night there; and they need no candle, neither light of the sun; for the Lord God giveth them light: and they shall reign for ever and ever" (Rev. 22:3-5). It is thrilling to know that apartments are free within the city, but entrance is strictly limited to those who have made prior arrangements to be accommodated.

It has become customary for people who intend to travel abroad to make arrangements whereby their needs in the new country will be supplied by money either transferred to a foreign bank or by checks carried by the travelers. People who neglect this important provision will be confronted by insurmountable problems. All are aware that nothing accompanies a soul into eternity. "We came into the world with nothing, and it is certain we can take nothing out." It therefore becomes necessary "to lay up treasure in heaven" before departure from this world. This can be done only by living faith in and service for the Savior. The need is urgent; wise men never procrastinate.

SCRIPTURE TEXT INDEX